WITHDRAWN

Saving the Mill

The amazing recovery of one of Japan's largest paper mills
following the 2011 earthquake and tsunami

Saving the Mill

The amazing recovery of one of Japan's largest paper mills
following the 2011 earthquake and tsunami

RYOKO
SASA

佐々涼子

Translated by
Tony Gonzalez

Japan Publishing Industry Foundation for Culture

Published by Japan Publishing Industry Foundation for Culture [JPIC],
3-12-3 Kanda-Jinbocho, Chiyoda-ku, Tokyo 101-0051, Japan

Saving the Mill: The amazing recovery of one of Japan's largest paper mills
following the 2011 earthquake and tsunami
Kami tsunage! Karera ga hon no kami o tsukutteiru:
Saisei Nipponseishi Ishinomaki Kôjô

Originally published in Japanese language by Hayakawa Publishing Corporation in 2014
English translation rights arranged with Hayakawa Publishing Corporation

Jacket and cover design: Hisanori Niizuma [gift inc.]
Jacket and cover photograph: Hiroshi Noguchi
Other photographs: Courtesy of the NPI Ishinomaki Paper Mill

As this book is published primarily to be donated to public libraries, educational institutions,
etc., commercial publication rights are available. For all enquiries regarding those rights,
please contact the publisher of the Japanese edition at the following address:
rights@hayakawa-online.co.jp

ISBN 978-4-916055-47-7
http://www.jpic.or.jp/japanlibrary/

We extend our special thanks to Nippon Paper Industries and the citizens of
Ishinomaki City for their cooperation in creating this book.

Introduction to the English edition of this book

I am delighted to have the opportunity to introduce the English translation of this book.

On March 11, 2011, the Great East Japan Earthquake triggered a massive tsunami that struck the Tohoku region. I am sure that those of you living overseas felt just as horrified as we did when you saw the video footage broadcast from Japan.

The Tohoku region was home to a large paper mill that suffered catastrophic damage from the tsunami. Its owner, Nippon Paper Industries, supplies about 40 % of all of Japan's paper used for publishing. This was both the company's main mill and a major source of employment in the region. While most thought that it would be impossible for the mill to recover, its manager declared, "We will resume production in six months." On that day, people began the laborious task of raking out debris by hand and removing rubble. In this most extreme of situations, what did people believe in? How did they live their lives? In what did they abandon hope? Where did they find hope? This book is a question, but it is also an answer. If you ever encounter problems, I hope that you will revisit this book. The people who live and breathe within its pages are bound to show you the way forward.

Ryoko Sasa

Prologue

At midnight on April 12, 2013, an unusual scene unfolded in front of bookstores throughout Japan. Long lines of people had gathered on the street, avid fans of the novelist Haruki Murakami eagerly awaiting the first chance to purchase his new book, *Colorless Tsukuru Tazaki and His Years of Pilgrimage.*

To commemorate the release, staff at the flagship store of one Tokyo bookseller had built a tower of books. The news media reported that they had piled up two hundred of the one thousand copies they had received the night before to a height of almost a meter and a half. The cover of *Tsukuru Tazaki* was decorated with colorful lines arranged neatly against a white background, making the tower look something like an out-of-season Christmas tree—a beautiful reminder of the arboreal origin of the paper that formed it.

As the tower was revealed, the waiting fans cheered and held up cell phone cameras to snap pictures. A television news crew arrived, and reporters thrust microphones into the faces of bookstore employees who seemed as excited about the release as their customers. The publishing industry was in the midst of a severe slump. This level of excitement over the release of a literary work was rare, adding to the celebratory tone of the night.

Equally thrilled about the day's events was a comparatively small group of people in northeast Japan's Tohoku region—employees at the Nippon Paper Industries (NPI) plant in the city of Ishinomaki. They were excited because the paper used to print *Tsukuru Tazaki* was manufactured on the plant's No. 8 paper machine, commonly referred to as "Machine 8," which along with the rest of the factory had been nearly destroyed in the Great East Japan Earthquake of 2011. The plant's recovery was something of a miracle.

Noriaki Sato is the team leader for Machine 8, and he loves paper. "Our paper has its quirks," he says. "When I go to a bookstore, I can pick out books printed on paper from our machine just by looking at them."

Paper does not bear the signature of its creators. The quality of the paper itself is their most eloquent signature, their proof of existence.

The basic materials for paper used in the publishing industry are woodchips from broadleaf trees like eucalyptus and from conifers like radiata pine. Making the paper used in glossy magazines, hardcover books, comics, or paperbacks requires delicate adjustments to the blend of woodchips. *Tsukuru Tazaki* was printed on a type of paper called "Opera Cream HO" created using only broadleaf chips, which are softer than conifer chips because of their shorter fibers. This softness makes premium paper like Opera Cream HO more pleasant to the touch than varieties that use a blend of chips.

One million copies of *Tsukuru Tazaki* were printed within seven days of its release, a new record for a literary work in Japan. This was both a dream come true and a nightmare for NPI—while the staff were of course thrilled about the additional sales, they began to wonder if they could keep up with demand.

Before production halted due to the earthquake and tsunami, the Ishinomaki plant churned out approximately one million tons of paper each year. By 2012 it had nearly recovered, and was producing approximately 850,000 tons. Today the main production unit, Machine N6, is operating at full capacity, and the plant manufactures paper night and day, without pause.

Few people know the story of what happened to make that possible.

At 2:46 PM on March 11, 2011, NPI's Ishinomaki plant was hit by a natural disaster on a scale rarely seen in history. On that day an enormous tsunami unleashed by a magnitude 9.0 earthquake struck the plant from three directions: the Pacific coast to the south, an industrial seaport to the west, and the Kitakami River to the east. According to the Japan Meteorological Agency, the tsunami that hit Ishinomaki was approximately 7.7 meters high. It flooded the plant with black water and clouds of dust, twisting rails for loading freight trains into tangles and knocking a forty-ton diesel engine onto its side.

The tsunami increased its momentum as it advanced across the land, swallowing the entire factory grounds in an instant. The waves then surged on to inundate a nearby residential area. Honking horns and the screams of those trying to evacuate could be heard as it flooded the streets. "So long as I live, I will never forget those sounds," one survivor said.

Inside the factory buildings, the tsunami reached heights of four meters. The freezing waters brought the wreckage of eighteen houses and around five hundred cars and trucks onto the grounds. As far as the eye could see, the landscape was covered in debris that just a few hours earlier had been the stuff of daily life for citizens in a prosperous community.

Workers at the Ishinomaki plant took refuge on nearby Mt. Hiyori. From there they watched their workplace and town disappear under the waves. When the waters receded, they shared a single thought: "It's over. There's no way the company will rebuild here." They had lost their homes, their families, their friends, and their livelihood. Many were so overcome with emotion that they couldn't move.

Yet their feelings were also complex. "No matter how bad things are, there's always someone else in the world who's worse off. We should be happy just to be alive," said one worker who lost his family in the disaster.

At the time of the disaster 162,822 people lived in Ishinomaki. Of those, 3,169 died in the earthquake and tsunami, and 793 remain missing. During the cleanup, 41 bodies were found on the paper plant's grounds.

I was a magazine reporter when the earthquake hit. Planned power outages in the Tokyo area—a measure to relieve shortages on the national electrical grid—were a constant reminder of what had happened, but a conversation with an editor at the magazine made the events feel somehow more real.

"We have a major problem," she said. "We're running out of paper. A huge factory in Ishinomaki makes most of our paper, but it got wiped out. We may need to reduce the number of pages in the next issue. I had no idea…"

I hadn't either. Writers and editors don't usually know much about the paper their stories are printed on.

I knew that the salmon I ate came from Norway and that my bananas came from the Philippines. I knew that Okinawa was famous for its sugarcane. But I had no idea where the paper used in our magazine came from. How embarrassing, to be in the publishing industry and not know that.

Apparently my editor felt the same way.

"Our job is based on paper, and we're always talking about how digital media will never replace it. Yet it takes a paper shortage for us to really notice the stuff."

She tried to smile, but there was clearly no humor behind it.

Three years have passed since then, and our lives have largely returned to normal. The lights are back on in our cities, the books are back in our bookstores, and we take it all for granted just as we did before the disaster. According to the *2014 Annual Report of Publishing Indices*, 77,910 different titles were published in Japan in 2013. Today we have no problem buying paper, which for a short period was such a precious commodity. The Tohoku region is starting to feel once again like a far-off place. Writers and editors have gone back to doing their jobs without thinking about where their paper comes from.

Human beings have an amazing ability to adapt to our environment. Disasters may crush us, but once they've passed we return to our everyday lives. This time, too, we're already starting to forget the unseen people who support our lives. It wasn't so long ago that the Ishinomaki plant was destroyed, yet few of us pause to think about what happened that day. Fewer still wonder about the people who made the plant's recovery possible.

One day about two years after the earthquake, I went to Ishinomaki. I wanted to learn what happened at the paper plant during and after the disaster and to write it down before we all forget.

The first thing I saw when I entered that giant building was the massive No. 8 paper machine, groaning as an unending river of paper gushed out of it. Occasionally somebody would walk by and glance at a flashing yellow light, but there were far fewer people around than I expected. Each crew consists of only four operators; for the most part, the machine does its work on its own.

Machine 8 is 111 meters long. As I watch, it's spinning a roll of paper so thick it looks like a pillar from a monument. When a roll is complete a giant cutter slices it off, and the next roll begins. The scale of everything around me is so large, I feel like I have somehow shrunk.

Machine 8 mainly produces finely coated and medium-grade papers. It was only when I heard the titles of some of the books printed on paper from this machine, however, that I understood just how closely it touches my life. The paper used for countless bestselling hardcover, paperback, and comic books is produced on this machine.

From off in the distance, Noriaki Sato approaches. He is the section chief of Manufacturing Division One, which is responsible for operating Machine 8. He's wearing a helmet, boots, and work overalls. He's suntanned, and surveys his surroundings with a keen gaze that marks him as a factory floor engineer.

When he reaches me he bows awkwardly, then leads me to a break room off to the side of the machine, where he hands me a canned coffee. I place a digital recorder on the desk and take out a notebook and pen to take notes.

NPI produces approximately 40% of the paper used for printing in Japan. I want to know more about the history of its main factory, both as a writer and a reader.

Noriaki begins to speak, something he does with conviction.

"When Machine 8 stops, so does the Japanese printing industry."

Ages and job descriptions of characters in this book are as they were at the time of the earthquake.

Table of Contents

Three percent of sales of the Japanese edition are being donated to the School Library Association of Japan, designated as a fund for purchasing books for elementary schools in Ishinomaki City.

The interior of this book was printed on 58.5 kg "Opera Cream HO" paper created on Machine 8 at the NPI Ishinomaki Paper Mill. Pages with color photographs were printed on 52 kg "b7 Bulky" paper, also created on Machine 8. The jacket and cover were printed on 86.5 kg "Aurora Coated" paper from NPI.

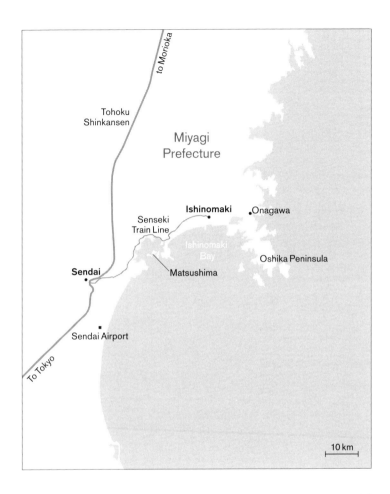

Ishinomaki and surrounding area

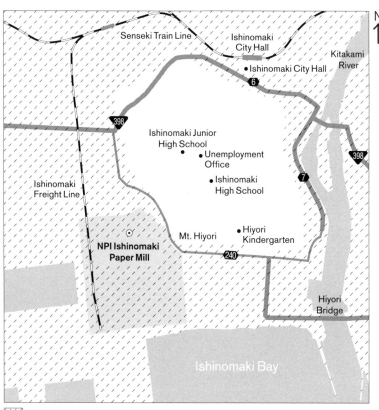

Ishinomaki city area

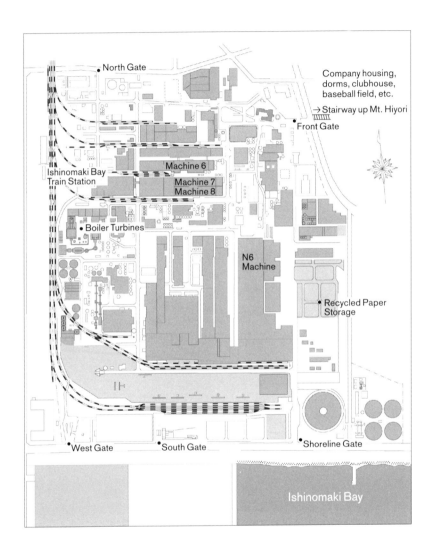

The NPI Ishinomaki Paper Mill, before the disaster

NPI produces around 40 % of the paper used for printing books and magazines in Japan, and the Ishinomaki plant is its main production facility.

CHAPTER 1

Destruction of the Ishinomaki Plant

20

1

To tell the tale of the Ishinomaki plant workers, we must begin on the day of the earthquake.

At 2:46 PM on March 11, 2011, Nippon Paper Industries (NPI) administrative director Yoshikatsu Murakami was meeting with city officials on the fifth floor of Ishinomaki City Hall. At the factory, he always wore overalls and safety boots, but that day he was in a suit and tie. Murakami is a serious man, known among colleagues for doggedly sticking to his decisions once they're made. The topic of the meeting that day was construction work underway at the industrial port just behind the factory.

Ishinomaki's city hall is located next to Ishinomaki Station, about 2.5 kilometers from the factory. It is surrounded by a commercial district that was once the city's main shopping area, but in the years leading up to the tsunami had lost customers to large malls and shopping centers in the suburbs. To combat this exodus of customers and attract tourists, the city had installed statues throughout the downtown area depicting popular characters from comics and cartoons.

The city hall building was originally a department store, and each floor has a spacious, open layout. From where Murakami sat he could see rows of civil servants working busily at their desks.

Suddenly, a chorus of buzzes and chirps rose up from those desks—alerts from an earthquake detection system sent to workers' cell phones. Murakami pulled out his own phone to call his wife Yuriko, to find out where she was and to make sure she was safe. As he was dialing, the building began to groan and shake. Murakami's coffee slid off the table and onto the leg of one of the men he was meeting with. Just as the man yelped from being splashed with hot coffee, the entire building began to oscillate from side to side.

The shaking was so strong that Murakami could not stand. The earthquake showed no sign of abating; rather, it grew increasingly powerful. He knelt on the floor and clutched the table, waiting for the earthquake to end. An air conditioning unit fell from the wall with a metallic crash, and pipes broke, spraying water into the room. A large bookshelf began to teeter. Workers rushed to prop it up, but the shaking was too intense. The first screams came from those diving out of the way as it toppled over.

The floor was lurching like a ship in a storm, tossing everyone first one way then the other. Murakami could do nothing but crouch where he was, watching out for the tables and chairs that slid about around him.

Everyone in the room had experienced earthquakes before, but this one was clearly different. When it finally stopped, Murakami rushed downstairs and out the door to the company van waiting for him in the parking lot.

"Get us to the factory," Murakami told his driver, Yoshinori Sugawara. With no traffic, the factory was only a five-minute drive from the city hall. The signals were all out, but no one was trying to evacuate yet, so they made good time.

During disasters, minutes can make the difference between life and death. If Murakami had acted any more slowly, it's likely that he and many of his employees would not be alive today.

"I've never felt anything like that before," he said to Sugawara. "Turn on the TV."

The driver hit the switch on a television mounted in the vehicle. The first reports of the disaster were already being broadcast. A tsunami warning had been issued, but that was nothing unusual. Few people in the disaster area paid it much mind.

Murakami did.

"I could feel it in my guts," he says. "I knew a tsunami was coming. Getting back to the plant was the only thing I could think about."

Many of the managers were absent that day, having traveled to Tokyo for a baseball game. The company team had been doing well for several years and was playing in the league tournament. Murakami had stayed behind to supervise the factory, adding to his feeling of responsibility.

He surveyed the town as the van sped through the streets. They passed the shopping district, the police station, a hospital, and a grave-yard. Other than the occasional car stopped by the side of the road and a few residents stepping outside to see what was going on, everything looked as it always did.

The weather had been clear that morning, but gray clouds had rolled in around noon. The temperature was around 5 °C—chilly for Tokyo-ites, but for residents of the region, where March snows are nothing unusual, the day held the promise of spring.

Murakami's wife Yuriko was a devoted fan of the company baseball team, and that day she and their daughter had joined the other employ-ees on their trip to watch the tournament. Murakami hoped they were far enough away to be safe.

His driver Sugawara, on the other hand, had a wife and elderly mother at home in town. Their house was located in a dense residen-tial area just beside the plant, near the Kitakami River. The wide, flat stretch of land facing the Pacific Ocean had been developed for hous-ing in the 1940s, around the time the pulp company that would even-tually become NPI began operations. There were 1,126 households in the area, with 2,716 people living in them.

A message appeared on the TV screen that gave Murakami chills: a four-meter tsunami had reached the Oshika Peninsula, less than thirty kilometers away. He tried several times to call someone on his cell phone, but the circuits were overloaded and he couldn't get through.

"Sugawara, have you managed to contact your family?"

Sugawara answered in his thick local accent: "Caught my wife at home. No luck with my mother." The worry in his voice was evident.

"Just drop me off at the gates, then go get your family," Murakami said. "Pick them up and head straight for Mt. Hiyori. No delays, okay? We'll meet you there."

"Thank you," Sugawara said, clutching the wheel but managing a shallow bow. He could feel something coming too. He was supposed to be at home on call that day, but had come to work to drive Murakami around. He later recalled this as a lucky stroke of fate.

NPI's Ishinomaki plant is huge. Its grounds cover approximately one square kilometer, with giant smokestacks poking up and shooting white clouds of steam into the air. The buildings tower above the other structures along the coastline, making the plant something of a landmark. The plant is in a geographically strategic location—approximately 55 kilometers northeast of the prefectural capital of Sendai, just a little over one hour by car. A dedicated rail line runs straight into the factory grounds, allowing the company to load and ship products directly to Tokyo without traffic delays.

The van finally pulled up to the factory gates.

Murakami jumped out and waved Sugawara off. He ran to the guard posted at the gate and told him to gather the other guards.

"A tsunami warning has been issued," he said. "Tell everybody here they have to evacuate. Don't leave anyone behind."

The staff had run emergency drills, so they knew what was expected of them. The guard picked up a microphone and broadcast an announcement throughout the plant: "A tsunami warning has been issued. Evacuate the premises immediately. I repeat, evacuate the premises immediately."

He and the other guards grabbed megaphones and headed off to assist with the evacuation.

At the time the Ishinomaki plant employed 514 full-time staff, and over 1,000 employees of affiliated companies also worked there on and off. The staff worked in three shifts, so personnel were constantly coming and going, but detailed logs recorded who was there at any given time. When the earthquake struck, 1,306 people were on site.

Murakami headed into the factory, determined to evacuate every one of them.

Not all the workers were willing to leave their posts right away; evacuation orders or no, many of them were performing tasks too complex to just drop and run off.

Engineering Division Chief Teruhiko Tamai, who was responsible for the plant's five boilers, has the stout build of a rugby player and a stalwart personality to match.

"I figured that even if a tsunami did come, the worst case scenario would be that we got our feet a little wet," he recalls. "We got tsunami warnings all the time, but I'd never actually seen one happen. The sea would rise a few centimeters, and that would be it. That was my image of a tsunami. I was much more worried about my turbines than about a glorified high tide."

When the earthquake hit, Tamai was in a meeting in a corner office in the turbine building. As soon as the shaking stopped, he headed straight for the power generator's central control panel to check on the boilers.

All five boilers were equipped with mechanisms that automatically shut them down in the event of a disaster, and four had done so. Only the heavy oil boiler was still running, and its operators were already working to turn it off manually.

Boilers burn fuel to heat water, converting it to high-pressure steam. That steam passes through turbines, which at the Ishinomaki plant measured up to six meters long. When large amounts of high-pressure steam press against the turbines' blades they spin, converting the thermal energy of the steam to rotational energy. That is passed to a power generator, which in turn converts it into electricity.

Boilers provided almost all the electricity powering the Ishinomaki plant. As the fifteen-ton turbines spun their shafts reached temperatures of around 500 °C, weakening them—if they stopped suddenly, they would collapse under their own weight. To prevent that, an electric motor had to keep them spinning until they cooled.

But the power was out. The workers would need to rotate the turbines manually until they could be safely stopped.

Turbines are made to order, and the newest one at the Ishinomaki plant—an N1 turbine—had cost around ¥2 billion (approximately US$20 million). If its shaft were damaged, a new one would have to be ordered. Cost aside, crafting the part would take two years.

At the time, the Ishinomaki plant used approximately 180,000 kWh of electricity, 92 % of which was produced on-site. If anything happened to the five boilers and turbines, the factory would cease to function.

Stopping a boiler by the books normally takes half a day. Engineers are not supposed to leave the machine during the process for any reason. To Tamai, damage to the boilers seemed far more likely than damage from a tsunami, so he got to work following the instructions in the manual for a safe shutdown.

"When I thought about what it would take to get it running again, sticking around doing things right seemed a lot better than just running off," he says. "But those were some pretty strong shakes, so as time passed I became increasingly nervous."

One of his team members went outside to see what was happening, and returned clearly shaken. "Everyone's clearing out," he reported. "We're one of the last groups here." The look in the man's eyes was enough to convince Tamai.

"Okay, let's go," he said.

The other members of the engineering division required no further persuasion. Thirty minutes had already elapsed since the earthquake hit. Their work site was on the side of the grounds closest to the ocean, almost a kilometer from the plant's front gates. Had they waited any longer, evacuation on foot would have been impossible.

Even within the plant, the seismic shocks were worse in some locations than others.

Chieko Motoki recalls that the shaking was so severe in the area where she and her team were working that they immediately feared for their lives. When the first tremors hit, the lights in their quality control laboratory went out. She screamed and dived under a workbench. It was all she could do to remain on her hands and knees and call out to the workers she was responsible for.

"Where is everyone? Is everybody okay?"

But no response came from the darkness.

Nearby, she could barely make out a crack that had opened in the factory floor. As she watched, the two sides of the crack jerked up and down with each shock, creating a thirty-centimeter drop between one side and the other. A stack of paper bales perched on the crack toppled in her direction. Had it landed on her, it would likely have killed her.

"We've got to get out of here!" she screamed.

She heard a faint reply from nearby: "I'm over here."

She crawled in the direction of the voice, and when she reached the terrified woman who had spoken they held each other and waited.

"I looked up at the ceiling, and saw that one end of the long fluorescent light fixture had become disconnected," she told me. "It looked like the other end would fall at any second, and I was sure that if it did it would hit one of us. Another team member was on the other side of the room, but all she could do was cry. I told her to pull herself together, that we would make it outside as soon as the shaking stopped. I didn't know what else to say."

Eventually the shaking did stop, and the women crawled out from under the tables where they had taken refuge. Still stunned, Chieko passed out coats to everyone and told them to run outside.

The building that housed the paper machine was made of steel-reinforced concrete to support the weight of the machinery, so the shaking there was less severe. Noriaki Sato, the manager of Machine 8, was able to stay calm and even crack a few jokes to defuse the tension. "Surf's up!" he shouted.

"Yeah, we got shaken up, but the machine looked like it was still in good shape," he told me. "We never even considered that a tsunami might be on its way. We probably wouldn't have evacuated if we hadn't seen everyone else running. We decided to go with them as much to avoid being left alone as anything else."

Outside, workers from the various buildings were gathering in groups. Spirits were generally high. After all, this wasn't the first powerful earthquake they had experienced.

In 2005, a magnitude 7.2 temblor occurred off the coast of Miyagi Prefecture. The earthquake was by no means small, but it did not produce a harmful tsunami. In 2010 an earthquake in Chile did cause a tsunami that reached Ishinomaki, but only at a height of 78 centimeters. It did not cause any damage.

In both cases the Japan Meteorological Agency had cried wolf with tsunami warnings. Company attempts to organize an evacuation following the Chile earthquake were hampered by the lack of a sense of urgency among employees. On this day too the workers were convinced that the worst had passed. Nevertheless, they gathered at the factory's main gate, figuring they might as well evacuate just in case. They headed to the nearest high ground: Mt. Hiyori.

More of a large hill than a mountain, Mt. Hiyori's peak is just 61 meters above sea level, its slopes are gentle enough that a quiet residential area has been built on them. At the top sit the company dormitory and clubhouse, as well as a baseball field and Ishinomaki High School. Most of the employees who gathered there had come as they were, not bothering to put on warmer clothing because they assumed they would be back at work soon—thirty minutes, tops. Some who worked in hotter parts of the plant were even wearing short sleeves, despite the cold. They chatted in groups, joking and laughing as they waited.

Taiji Takahashi was a contributor to the factory newsletter, so he was in the habit of bringing his camera to company events. That day he had been working in an old wooden office that creaked and groaned when the earthquake hit, sending a two-hundred-kilogram printer sliding across the floor as if it were on rollers. When the shaking stopped he used a long pole as a lever to move the printer back into position, but a strong aftershock soon displaced it again. That was when he decided it was time to run.

On his way out he passed a small shrine on the factory grounds. Next to it grew a zelkova tree that was often crowded with local crows. That day, however, there was not a bird to be seen. When Takahashi noticed this, a lump formed in his throat. "Things just didn't feel right," he says. "It was like a portent that something bad was coming."

He ran back to his office to get his camera, intending to take photos of the evacuation. He also put on a helmet and a warm coat, and grabbed the bag that contained his driver's license and cell phone. He jumped on one of the bicycles used for getting around the plant and pedaled toward the front gates.

He shot some photos of the last groups of evacuating workers, many wearing helmets but walking casually toward the evacuation site. No one seemed to be in a hurry—it was as if they were out for a casual stroll. He stopped for a few more shots of the now empty grounds. His sense of danger was increasing, however, so he quickly continued on. What had earlier been a light drizzle had turned to snow, and the cold wind blew the flakes against his cheeks.

In front of the gates near the guard station, the earthquake had forced groundwater up to form a thirty-centimeter-deep puddle. Somebody had laid a ladder over it to serve as a bridge. Everyone except the guards seemed to be gone already, and the factory grounds were deathly silent. Taiji turned back to snap a few final photos through his telephoto lens.

"Okay, now it's *really* time to get out of here," he told himself.

He started to cross the street that ran in front of the factory. On the other side a narrow concrete staircase wound up through the trees toward Mt. Hiyori, where his coworkers would be waiting. The one-lane road was congested with cars, their drivers trying to distance themselves from the ocean just a few hundred meters to the south. Traffic was at a standstill.

Just as Taiji stepped between the stopped cars, black water washed silently over his feet. He jumped with surprise. "It's here," he thought. He dashed between the cars toward the staircase. As he ran he glanced at the drivers in their cars. They were all facing away from the ocean.

By this time Murakami had led a group of employees halfway up the hill. The road that led to the top was crowded with a long line of unmoving taxis and private vehicles. Murakami stopped at the company picnic area to call roll and let everyone rest. He told them to wait there for the time being.

Snow began to fall from the low, gray clouds, and those who weren't dressed for the weather shivered. They had been outside for over thirty minutes, already longer than they had expected, and many began to ask if they could leave.

"I left my house and car keys back at the office. Okay if I go back and get them?"

"Can I run back and grab a coat?"

"I haven't been able to get hold of my family. I'd kinda like to cut out and see if they're okay…"

Murakami refused them all.

"Nobody goes back down the mountain. No exceptions."

Some people began to grumble, complaining that they would catch cold or that Murakami was overstepping his bounds. Some of the workers were older than Murakami and didn't appreciate taking orders from a mid-level manager. Murakami remained firm, knowing that if he let even one person go, many more would follow.

"Company orders," he said. "Everybody stays right here."

A few people complained, but nobody defied the order once it was given.

"I didn't want to be such a drillmaster, but it was the only way to keep everyone safe," he says.

He had no control over the local residents who had climbed the hill with them, however. One by one they started to leave. Among those heading back was a friend of Murakami's. Murakami tried to stop him.

"I'm sure a tsunami is coming this time. It's dangerous down there. You really should stay."

"I'm just going to check on my house," his friend said. "No worries, I'll be right back."

Murakami would never forget the sight of his friend heading back down the hill. It was the last time he ever saw him.

At 3:48 PM, approximately one hour after the earthquake, the people gathered on the hill heard a strange rumbling sound. Murakami looked out toward the ocean and saw what looked like a black wall with a cloud of dust floating over it. The wall pushed into the town. It knocked the lower stories of homes out from under their upper levels, which dropped into the water below and floated away.

In what felt like the next instant, Murakami saw water rising toward where he stood.

"Tsunami! Run!" he shouted.

He looked down at the base of the hill, where a long line of cars still waited. Their drivers either hadn't noticed the tsunami or were frozen in fear. Not a single person got out.

"Forget your cars! Get up here!"

But no matter how much Murakami yelled, nobody moved.

Takahashi the cameraman was still running up the stairs. He glanced back and saw the debris-laden tsunami bearing down on him. Almost unable to believe what he was seeing, he paused just long enough to snap a few hasty shots. The wave continued to build and swell, swallowing everything in its path.

The black water was beginning to engulf the cars stuck in traffic in front of the factory gates. Drivers began futilely honking their horns. Takahashi watched as the wave washed over them.

From above, Murakami watched a wave slam a car against the base of the mountain. A man stumbled out with a dazed expression on his face. The car behind him was pushed up the mountain too, but not quite far enough—as the water receded, it pulled the car back out into the ocean.

The tsunami pressed on in a series of waves, each higher than the last. Murakami watched the water lift a large truck. He caught a glimpse of the driver's face moments before the waves smashed the truck into a house that had been ripped from its foundation. "Like toys in a bathtub," he thought. "Who'd have thought something like that would float…"

He shook his head, trying to clear it of such inappropriate thoughts, but the situation wasn't one that his mind could accept as reality.

Kazuya Shimura, an employee in the factory's procurement division, watched the tsunami approach from the top of the hill. He too saw the ocean form an eerie black wall that knocked down houses one after another as it crawled forward. He saw utility poles snap from their bases, whipping power lines that shot sparks. A medley of grim sounds reached his ears: the crackling of downed transformers, a ripping noise like cloth being torn, the screech of grinding metal, honking horns, the whistle of propane gas from dislocated tanks, and above all else, screams for help. In the distance, he heard soft booms from something exploding. He smelled gasoline. Just below him, the sea formed an enormous whirlpool that dragged houses, automobiles, and people under the water. The snow fell on a world drained of color.

"It was…unreal, like being in a nightmare where everything was shifted around," he said. "If I looked to the left or to the right, everything was so familiar. But when I looked down there was the ocean, in a place it shouldn't be."

I asked him what it felt like to face a scene that defied imagination.

"Some of the women there were crying and screaming. I guess they were the ones in better touch with their emotions. I had completely shut down. I didn't feel fear or sadness. At one point I noticed that I was laughing, not that I found anything humorous in the situation. I wondered, is this what people do at times like this? Laugh?"

"It's too dangerous here! We need to move to higher up!"

Murakami gathered groups of employees who were standing halfway up the hill, too stunned to continue. Lower down was a building the company used for indoor baseball practice. Someone had opened it up to allow around five hundred people to take shelter inside, but those evacuees were now streaming out in search of higher ground. There was no longer any hint of joviality. The people climbing the mountain looked pale and stricken.

A taxi with a huge dent in its bumper came rolling up one of the streets that cut through the hillside residential area. It had clearly rammed the car ahead of it to make room to escape. No other cars followed.

Murakami did what he could to ensure that his employees were safe. He saw that Tamai and the others in charge of the boilers had escaped. So had the cameraman Takahashi, who told him, "If anybody was behind me, they didn't make it."

Murakami knew that there were indeed people behind Takahashi—at a minimum, his coworker Takashi Sato and the four security guards, who had been directing the evacuation. He could picture them running through the plant grounds, looking for stragglers and telling them to get out. It was harder to imagine them beneath the waves, though he knew what the tsunami must have done to the factory.

He peered through the snow, trying to find the plant, but all he could see was debris floating in muddy water. He couldn't even tell where the front gates should be. He let out a soft groan.

He headed to the evacuation shelter at the top of the hill, which was now overflowing with local residents. He worked his way through the crowd, checking faces. But no matter how much he searched, he couldn't find Takashi or any of the guards.

2

The skies above Tokyo were clear and sunny that day.

NPI president Yoshio Haga was at his desk on the sixteenth floor of the company's headquarters. His corner office looks straight down on the Imperial Palace, with the Budokan Arena off to the right.

The entire building shuddered when the earthquake hit. Haga knew instantly that this time, something was different. The building began to sway and the shaking continued on and on, far longer than any earthquake he'd experienced before. His desk began sliding toward the window, closer with each shock. He was struck by an unfamiliar fear of heights. What if his window shattered and he was hurled to the ground below?

When the shaking finally ceased, he gingerly approached the window to look outside. He saw a crowd streaming out of a nearby event hall. He later learned that the ceiling had collapsed, killing two people.

He went to his secretary's office.

"Where was the epicenter?"

"Somewhere in the Tohoku region, they're saying."

NPI had two factories in Miyagi Prefecture, one in Ishinomaki and the other in Iwanuma. Earthquakes had damaged both in the past.

"Find out whatever you can," he said.

Neither cell phones nor landlines were working, however, so they had no way of determining the situation. Unable to obtain information any other way, Haga joined his secretary and chief of sales in front of a television.

It wasn't long before newscasters began giving reports of a tsunami. Video footage showed the wave approaching Sendai Airport and washing over airplanes. Another clip showed a black wave racing over rice paddies in Natori city. Haga and his staff found themselves unable to speak, only sighing or groaning from time to time.

Haga was anxious to hear news of Ishinomaki, but none came. He had worked as a manager at the plant for five years and knew every inch of it. He recalled a story an older coworker there had told him:

"Once when I was a kid there was this earthquake in Chile. Afterward, the Kitakami River just sort of drained away. All that was left were millions of fish flopping around in the mud. A bunch of people took buckets down to the riverbed and started filling them with fish. Shame to waste 'em all, right? So all these people are down there with their buckets of fish, their eyes down on the muck, looking to grab just one more, just one more… When all that water came back as a big tsunami it swept away every last one of them."

New video footage and damage reports were coming in constantly, but still none from Ishinomaki.

"Have you gotten hold of anybody?" Haga asked his secretary.
"The phone lines are all still down."
"No luck here, either," another staff member said. "We've been going through the employee roster, but none of the numbers we have are getting through."
"What about the satellite phone?"
His secretary shook his head. "The circuits must be overloaded."
"Well I don't care how you get the information, but find out what's going on. I need a report on everyone's safety and what kind of damage we're looking at."
By now Haga was sure the tsunami had hit Ishinomaki. The only question was how bad the situation was.
When he finally received word of what was happening, it came from a surprising source: the sales division of NPI's Osaka office. While communication circuits were overloaded in the Tokyo area, things weren't quite as bad farther west.

To: Yoshio Haga
From: Masahiko Kondo, NPI Kansai Office
Date: 11 Mar 2011, 4:33 PM
Subject: Ishinomaki status (first reports)

Sending you some information we got about earthquake damage to the Ishinomaki plant. At around 4 PM we finally got through to the cell phone of a Mr. Yoshida at the products division there. He was on his way to pick up his child from school. Here's what he reports:

A 3 to 4 m tsunami hit the Ishinomaki plant, which is currently covered in water, cars, and debris.
From the look of things, getting it functional again is going to

take a long time.
Employees have taken refuge on a nearby mountain.
The Ishinomaki train station is flooded and covered with a
mountain of junk.

Mr. Yoshida was in a near panic, so that's all we could really
get out of him. More as we hear it.

The email had a photo attached, sent via the Iwakuni plant in Yamaguchi Prefecture.

"What's this?" Haga asked.

"They say it's the traffic signal in front of the plant gates."

At first Haga thought it must be some kind of mistake. The traffic signal should have been four or five meters above ground, but only twenty or thirty centimeters showed above the water.

"So… The entire gate is *under water*?"

That could only mean one thing—the entire plant was destroyed.

The Osaka office continued to contact Ishinomaki as often as possible and forwarded the information to Tokyo.

"What about the staff there?" Haga asked.

"Five are still missing."

"Tell them to let us know as soon as they hear anything."

"Will do."

The company had never faced a situation like this. The faces of coworkers from the Ishinomaki plant flashed through Haga's mind.

All the trains in Tokyo had stopped, paralyzing transportation. Haga told those employees with homes or family nearby to go check on them. Those who remained were to do everything they could to gather accurate information about what was going on. Haga also told them to set up a special team by 10:00 AM the next day that would be dedicated to dealing with the damage. He and most of the Tokyo employees spent the night in the office, gathering information.

In Ishinomaki the snow had stopped, but night was rapidly approaching.

Murakami and the other NPI employees were exhausted from the cold and the shock of the tsunami. They split up to take shelter where they could, some at an unemployment office on the hill, others at a nearby junior high school.

Foremost in everyone's mind was the safety of family members. With cell phones still not working and the water lapping the base of the mountain, it was impossible for most to go searching. Some who lived in areas where the water was relatively shallow waded off to look for parents, spouses, and children, despite the cold. The rest could only pray for the safety of their loved ones.

What had once been the city was now an expanse of debris-laden water. Thin clouds covered the sky, and the sun was rapidly growing weaker; it would set at 5:37 PM that day. The night that followed would be unlike any the town had ever seen.

Murakami was doing what he could to help people near the dormitory. He later recalled his memories of those hours:

The smell was just awful. It was the smell of disaster. Burning trees, plastic... even people... On that day and the next I was able to help maybe fifty people, but I watched twice as many die. There was nothing we could do to save them.

Fires started breaking out everywhere. Small ones at first—a bucket of water would've been enough to put them out. But it was all floating debris, out of reach. People were trying to climb up on the stuff that was floating around, but most of it would sink when they did. There were dozens of people up on roofs, calling for help, but there was no way to get to them. Most of them were elderly and unable to get to us either.

One side of Mt. Hiyori is covered in concrete blocks to prevent erosion. We saw several people trying to climb them to get out of the water. They would stick their fingers into cracks and hang on for dear life, but the cold must have drained their strength. They'd make it halfway up, then fall back into the water. We would call to them and point to the stairs nearby, but the debris prevented them from getting there. We really wanted to help them, but we didn't have any ropes or ladders. In the end, not a single person managed to make the climb.

I guess around twenty waves came that night. More, some people say. When the first wave drew back and the next one came, it shorted out a lot of the automobiles that had washed up. They would throw sparks, which would land on bits of broken houses and start fires. They were small at first, but when new waves came they would shuffle things around, causing the fires to spread. So as the night went on, the fires grew larger.

Later I heard people complaining that the fire department did nothing to save their homes, that they spent all their efforts on Mt. Hiyori. But if the hill had caught fire, we'd have had nowhere to run. I mean, we were surrounded by water, right? There were probably ten thousand people up on that hill. I can't imagine what it would have been like if a major fire broke out.

I remember a neighbor found me and said, "I just got a text from my wife. She's trapped in our house and needs help." We could even see the house from where we were, but we had no way to get there. Someone from the fire department passed by, and we told him about it. He took off his helmet and protective gear and tied a rope around his waist. He said, "I'm going to swim out to the house. If you see me get snagged on anything, please pull me back as best you can."

When he got to the house it had collapsed, and nobody answered his calls. He didn't give up though. He made his way in, crawling through a window or something. After a while we heard him yelling, "I found her!"

She'd been caught in the wreckage, pinned from the waist down. "Pull the rope!" the firemen yelled, and we pulled with all our might. She was screaming and moaning, but she finally came free. When we finally got her up on land, she had broken bones all along the right side of her body. The firemen radioed a hospital, but they said, "All our beds are full, and the place is filled with mud. Even if you bring her here, we won't have a clean place to put her. She's better off at whatever facilities you have there. Maybe NPI has a good place."

Stuff like that was happening all over. There was a guy covered in mud who'd just barely managed to keep his mouth above water until we could pull him out. Another guy who'd lost a hand… We saved a lot of people, but there were so many we couldn't help. I can still see them when I close my eyes.

From his post on the hilltop Murakami could hear screams of pain coming from the islands of floating rubbish. Some people yelled out, "I'm over here!" or "I need help!" Others could only manage to moan or wail. He couldn't even see most of them because they were trapped inside clumps of debris or floating houses.

Murakami was tortured by their closeness, just a short swim away. But he knew he wouldn't last long in the cold water. He was far more likely to become a casualty himself than to successfully rescue anyone.

The smell of spilled chemicals became increasingly strong, making everyone nervous. A spark set off a booming explosion, and an eerie orange fireball ignited surrounding debris. The wind whipped the blaze higher, producing thick clouds of oily smoke. Murakami stood there, powerless, thinking of all those people trapped in a hell of burning trash and icy water.

Please, make it stop, he thought.

Shimura from the procurement division made his way as far down the hill as he could to have a look at the situation there. He immediately wished he hadn't. Several people, young and elderly, were clinging to a roof that was floating nearby, waiting to be rescued. A few NPI employees had waded into the water in an attempt to reach them.

Shimura wanted to help, but his legs wouldn't move. For the first time in his life he found himself literally paralyzed with fear. Oil slicks had formed on the water's surface, some of them ablaze. At the factory he had often participated in danger assessment exercises, and he couldn't shake the image of himself going to help but ending up covered in flames. His wife was pregnant with their first child, due that September. *I can't die here, not now*, he thought.

But just as he couldn't bring himself to head out into the water, he couldn't turn his back on his coworkers, either. So he just stood there, unable to move. He managed to call out several times to the people on the roof. "You've got to get over here! It's going to catch fire!" They were likely as terrified as he was, however, and stayed where they were. Even the younger ones couldn't work up the nerve to jump into the water.

Shimura made his way to the water's edge, where he helped pull up a few survivors. He called to those on the roof again in an effort to wipe away some of the guilt he felt for not doing more. Eventually the fires became so intense that he and the others on land had to back away. *They're dead*, he thought, looking at the figures on the roof. *They're dead.*

He took several steps backward up the path. Unable to watch any more, he turned away and climbed back up the hill.

Hiroyuki Suzuki looks much younger than his 43 years, but as branch manager of the plant's labor union and representative for its six hundred members, he has earned the trust of workers both younger and older than himself. Born and raised in Ishinomaki, he began working at the NPI plant alongside his father after graduating from high school.

Suzuki and his family had lived in company housing for many years, but company regulations allowed that only until the age of fifty, so they had recently built a house on Mt. Hiyori. The family moved into their new home just six days before the earthquake hit.

Suzuki took many photographs of the view below the house to commemorate the move. His pictures show an expanse of red and blue roofs splashed with the magenta of camellia bushes growing in yards. Beyond this placid, homey scene, the NPI plant sends up billows of pure white steam, just as Suzuki grew up seeing.

All of that was gone now. The tsunami had nearly reached his house, and an ocean of wreckage took the place of the view he had loved so much.

After making his way back home he and his neighbors helped five or six people out of the water. All were elderly, half-drowned, and weak, so he quickly moved them into his house. Their health was deteriorating rapidly, however. One moaned and lost control of his bowels. Another stopped moving entirely. Suzuki went outside to look for help and found a city employee who happened to be passing by. He told him about the elderly people, and not long after, a car came by and picked them up. Suzuki never found out what happened to them after that.

Just ten meters down the hill from his home was the borderline between life and death. The winds blowing off the water were so hot he was afraid his house would catch fire.

Late that night a fire crew arrived. "We noticed you have a new house there," one of them said. "Want us to spray it down, try to keep the flames off?"

Suzuki nodded, deeply touched. Even in this situation, the firemen were thinking only of how they could help others.

The firefighters had gathered what hoses they could find on the hill and were using the high school pool to fill their tanks. There was no longer any water pressure in the area, however, and their efforts could not match the inferno that surrounded them.

"What about your home?" Suzuki asked. "Is your family okay?"

"We got orders to move out as soon as the earthquake hit," the firemen replied. "I've been working since then, so I can't say for sure, but I'm pretty sure my home is gone. I just hope my family made it out. But for now, protecting lives and property in the city is my job."

They heard a woman shouting near the fire. "We're over here! Please, somebody help!" A man groaned wordlessly and a child screamed.

"It's so dark out here that we can't find people trapped in debris. Sometimes we see flames shoot up and hear the screams of people being burned alive. It's horrible. The screams grow louder and louder, peak, then just kind of fade away. I even heard a child die that way, somewhere out in the darkness. There was nothing we could do to help."

A woman stumbled into Suzuki's yard, propped up by an elderly parent on each arm. Leaving them, she went back, as close to the flames as she could bear, and began calling her child's name.

"Mommy's here! I'm over here! Where are you? Please, answer me! Where are you?"

She continued to call out, over and over, until she grew hoarse.

"Where are you? Where *are* you? Please, please answer me!"

Her parents went to her to give what comfort they could.

Suzuki looked out into the darkness, thinking, *I should have forced them to come with me.* His aunt and uncle, both in their eighties, lived in the town below. He had driven to their home immediately after the earthquake.

"They've issued a tsunami warning. I came to pick you up. C'mon, let's go!"

But they wouldn't hear of it.

"We're fine, we're fine. You get back to work," they said.

"Well, if it looks like one's really coming you two go upstairs, okay?"

he said, and left.

That was the last time he saw them alive—their home was swallowed by the wave.

"We couldn't see the water," said one employee who spent the night at the unemployment office. "But we knew the town was burning. The light coming through the windows was orange all night long."

He lost his cousin that night, and says he never wants to experience anything like that again.

"There's not much you can do, other than respect your fear," he says. "You have to trust that friends and family will be safe, and get to higher ground yourself."

Another employee talked about the rumors flying that night.

"Everybody was talking about how the plant must've burned down. I mean, the place was filled with flammable chemicals, so how could it not? Afterwards they found around five hundred automobiles on the plant grounds, including two hundred that had washed in from outside. It's a miracle the whole place didn't go up in flames. If it had, there's no way they would've rebuilt."

3

By the next morning, the water had receded enough for Murakami and a small group of employees to walk down the hill and check on the factory. They were startled by how quiet the town was. They managed to locate the sign that had stood next to the factory gates, but now it was surrounded by enormous piles of crushed cars, toppled traffic signals, and debris from demolished houses that the waves had pushed into scattered islands. Some were topped with a thin layer of snow. For a while the entire landscape was motionless. Presently, though, they noticed an elderly woman walking unsteadily toward them, picking her way through the debris.

"It's dangerous down here," Murakami called out to her. "Come join us, we'll take you up the hill where it's safer."

But the woman did not answer. Her expression was blank, her eyes unfocused. She seemed to be mumbling something as she walked. They couldn't make out what she was saying at first, but as she got closer her words became clear.

"He's gone… He's gone…"

Her random stumbling took her in another direction, and she passed out of sight. The area once again fell silent.

During the cleanup in the days that followed, they found a large truck that had washed onto the plant grounds. The body of an elderly man was stretched across the hood, seemingly uninjured. Next to him was an area free of snow in the shape of another body lying tightly against him. Apparently he and his wife had spent the night on the hood, using residual heat from the truck's engine to stay warm, but he had succumbed to hypothermia.

"I wonder what happened to the guards," Murakami said, scanning the grounds. It was impossible to know who was safe and who wasn't. He tried to create a mental list of those he had seen reach safety, but he no longer trusted his memory, and reports from others were equally questionable. Nobody had slept, nobody had eaten, and everyone was close to collapsing from exhaustion.

Takahashi the cameraman spent the night in his car, which he kept in a parking lot on Mt. Hiyori.

"It was freezing cold, but the car was almost out of gasoline," he said. "I'd run the engine just long enough to heat things up a little, then turn it off and try to get some sleep. It was pretty rough around dawn. Cars don't do a very good job of retaining heat."

The scene at the bottom of the hill was like something from the end of times, but above it stretched a beautiful blue sky—a stark contrast with the chilling gray of the day before. It was warmer too, so warm that under better circumstances Takahashi would have been daydreaming of early cherry blossoms.

"It was almost painful," he said. "At any other time I would've gone around saying what a beautiful day it was. It was the kind of weather you wished you could bottle up and sell."

Looking down from the hill, he saw that the tsunami had erased those parts of the town closest to the ocean. He wondered what had become of his home, which was on the west side of the factory. *I guess that's gone too*, he thought.

He was struck by an irresistible urge to photograph the area around the boilers. He had a bad leg, and there was nowhere in the plant to take refuge, so he knew that if another tsunami came it would mean death. Even so, he grabbed his camera and started down the hill.

Suzuki surveyed his house, which had miraculously escaped destruction during the fires the night before. The area just below him was still inundated. Across the water he could see an apartment building with black holes where windows used to be. He heard a cry for help coming from one of them.

He heard a thumping sound and looked up to see a helicopter hovering overhead like a dragonfly. "Over there! Someone needs help!" he shouted, gesturing wildly at the apartments. But the helicopter did not attempt to land. Suzuki imagined the unseen person in the apartments calling to him for help but getting no response, mirroring his futile attempts to call down the helicopter.

The voice calling for help grew weaker as the day went on. The next morning, he heard nothing at all.

At one point an elderly man wandered through Suzuki's yard. Suzuki watched from a window as the man paused at the edge of the property to gaze at the destroyed town. After staring for a while, the man unzipped his pants and began urinating, pointing his yellow arc of urine into the flooded city below. Suzuki went out into the yard. The area this man was using as a toilet had until a day earlier been a mosaic of red and blue roofs, with laundry fluttering on lines in the yards between them.

Suzuki spoke to the man. "Hey, that water you're pissing into? There's still people in there, cold and miserable and waiting to be helped."

The man's eyes widened with shock and embarrassment. "You're right," he said. "I shouldn't have done that." He bowed and walked away.

Because dangerous chemicals had been stored at the plant and might now be leaking, NPI's management instructed employees not to return for the time being. Besides, they had no idea what else the tsunami might have left behind. Nonetheless, a team of five employees decided to scout the grounds and look for survivors. Shimura was among them.

The water had not yet fully receded, so the five picked their way across high mounds of rubble. The destruction was so extensive that they didn't know where to begin. Just fifty or sixty meters in, they were forced to turn back.

"When we saw how bad things were, not one of us thought the plant would ever reopen," Shimura says.

The ground floors of all the buildings were flooded with muddy water, and a layer of debris two meters thick covered the grounds. The power was out, so the buildings were dark inside. They had no idea what might lie within.

They managed to find a first aid kit and salvage a pot from an office kitchen. They turned back bearing these precious items.

"We saw a safe that must've weighed a hundred kilograms embedded in a ceiling," Suzuki says. "We just gave up. We weren't equipped to deal with stuff like that. In front of one of the buildings we found a man wearing just his underwear lying facedown in the mud, dead. There were seven more in cars, all dead, all facedown."

Employees gathered at the clubhouse located partway up Mt. Hiyori to form an emergency support team. The elegant building had formerly been used to entertain visiting VIPs.

The team started by drawing up a list of employees whose safety they were able to confirm. The only people not on the list were the four guards and Sato from the administration division. They scoured evacuation sites in search of the missing five, but with no success. Several people told the emergency team that they had seen the men looking for stragglers during the evacuation. All the evidence suggested they had not escaped. A grim mood filled the clubhouse office.

"After everything they did to help us…"

Reluctantly, the team notified Tokyo headquarters that five employees were missing.

More than anyone else, Murakami was wracked with guilt. When the evacuation began he and Sato had each observed what the other was doing, and by unspoken agreement had divided up the duties. Murakami would lead employees up the hill, while Sato would remain below to deal with the situation on the grounds. The expression on Sato's face at the time was burned into Murakami's memory. "Don't worry, I've got things under control," he seemed to be saying. Murakami hadn't even thought about the danger involved.

Murakami noticed that the other people in the office had stopped talking and were staring fixedly toward the door, as if they had seen a ghost. When he turned in the same direction, he saw that several people had entered the room. At first he couldn't tell who they were. But after a pause, he let out a cry of joy.

It wasn't a ghost they'd seen, it was Takashi Sato. Behind him stood the four guards.

"Takashi! You're alive!"

Murakami wiped tears from his eyes. "So that's everyone, right? Everybody's safe?"

But this time Sato began to tear up. He spoke in a voice so soft everyone leaned forward to hear him.

"Not everybody," Sato said. "There was an assistant fire chief helping us with the evacuation, but we lost track of him. We tried to find him before we left, but…"

Everyone in the room smiled, and Murakami pounded Sato on the shoulder.

"Don't worry," Murakami said. "He's up here, safe with us. He came up the hill just as the tsunami hit."

Sato collapsed forward in relief, propping himself up with his hands on his knees. After catching his breath he looked up, his grim expression gone.

"Well then, I guess we all made it," he said, smiling.

*The factory gates immediately
following the disaster*

CHAPTER 2

Survivors

What happened to Takashi Sato between the time the tsunami hit and the moment he walked into the makeshift emergency command office on Mt. Hiyori?

Sato is a small, unassuming, not particularly athletic man. As he told me his story in his quiet voice, at times I found it hard to believe what I was hearing.

Like so many others, Sato did not even consider the possibility of a tsunami following the earthquake. He does remember one warning, however, delivered from a coworker years before: "When a strong quake comes the drainage pumps stop and water overflows. That can kick manholes up into the air, so be careful."

Sato's main duties at NPI were related to human resources and labor relations. In the event of a disaster he was responsible for helping form a response team and aiding in plant evacuations.

When the earthquake subsided, Sato made his way back to his office, but found it empty—everyone had already evacuated. He looked for the satellite phone, but it wasn't in its usual place. Somebody must have taken it with them. Sato put on his coat, knowing it was going to be a long day.

Outside, he saw a group of employees walking toward the front gates. He passed them as he jogged off in that direction himself.

When he got there, he saw that some flooding had occurred, just as his coworker had warned. The guards were laying a ladder across the large puddle to form a bridge. Sato grabbed a megaphone from the guard station and shouted instructions to the people heading his way.

"You can pass by over here! This way, please!"

A radio had been left on in the guard station, broadcasting the news.

"This just in—we have received reports of a tsunami developing in the Onagawa River. Eyewitnesses say it's high enough to reach the eaves of houses—"

Sato locked eyes with one of the guards and lifted the megaphone again.

"Hurry! This way, please! Move as quickly as you can!"

Still, Sato remained optimistic about the situation. "Even after those first reports about the Onagawa River, I didn't really think a big tsunami would reach us. There's a peninsula between here and there, and I couldn't imagine a tsunami large enough to wash over that. At the same time—and I couldn't tell you why I thought this—I figured that even if a tsunami did come we'd just have to relocate a couple meters higher. I was picturing a volleyball net, thinking we needed to get higher than that."

The last group finally passed through the gates. Only six people remained on the plant grounds: Sato, the head guard, the three guards who worked under him, and an assistant fire chief.

Checking the emergency gear he had brought with him, Sato noticed that his flashlight wasn't working. He clicked the switch several times, but the bulb remained dark.

"The batteries must be dead," the head guard said. "I'll go get some fresh ones."

He headed off to a supply cabinet. One guard remained in the guard station, reading an emergency evacuation notice over the broadcasting system. The fireman stepped just outside the gate to take a look around. Everyone else stood near the guard station, waiting for the head guard to return.

All the machinery in the plant had stopped, and the grounds were strangely silent. Sato scanned his surroundings. The only person he could see was the head guard walking back toward them, batteries in hand.

I guess we got everybody out, he thought.

The silence was suddenly shattered by the sound of several cars honking their horns. When he turned toward the road, he saw cars being washed backward down the street. He froze for a moment, unable to process what was happening, but snapped to when the head guard let out a cry.

"Tsunami!"

Sato turned toward the ocean. In the distance he saw a row of large trees shaking unnaturally, and behind them an enormous cloud of dust. A strange rumbling sound reached his ears. Sato willed himself to run. The guards followed.

At first he headed for the thermomechanical pulping building, but it was on a road leading directly to an ocean-facing gate. If they ran there from the guard station, they would be heading straight for the tsunami. Sato could already see water rushing toward him. He changed course and headed for a stairway leading up to the inspection window of a silo used to store raw materials. The guards scrambled up a ladder attached to a different tank.

Sato watched through the metal latticework of the stairs as the tsunami rushed in below him. Black waves formed spinning vortices of cars and debris, and a cool breeze blew up from below. He had run forty or fifty meters to reach the stairway; had he stumbled even once, he would be underwater now. He knew he had experienced a brush with death, yet none of it seemed real.

Some of the cars swirling below him still had drivers inside. A few stuck their heads out the windows, looking down at the water. All of them gripped their steering wheels.

"Forget your cars! Get up here!" he shouted, but none did. He watched as they floated away.

He could see his office, a wooden one-story structure that opened in a U shape toward the sea. Debris began accumulating between its arms. Eventually, the pressure became so great that the middle gave way. The building's framework remained for a time, but soon even that disintegrated into the surging, turbid water. Sato watched as his workplace of so many years vanished without a trace.

He realized he had lost track of the assistant fire chief, also named Sato. He shouted his name at the top of his lungs.

"Mr. Sato! Mr. Sato, are you there?"

He saw a nearby tree shaking, and someone called from it.

"I'm here! I'm over here!"

It wasn't the fireman, however, but a young man he didn't know. The tree he clung desperately to was around thirty meters from Sato's tower. He climbed down from the tree and splashed through the water to join Sato.

He said he was a worker at the nuclear power plant in Onagawa, and that he had managed to escape from his car after it washed onto the NPI factory grounds. His arms and legs had been severely injured. His workman's overalls were soaked in seawater and blood, and he grimaced with pain. His face was blue from shock, cold, and blood loss. Sato took the towel that was wrapped around his neck and did what he could to stop the bleeding.

"Hang in there. We'll get you help."

The young man nodded. He crouched on the stairs and leaned against the silo. A layer of wet snow was accumulating on his clothes, hair, and face.

Sato looked over at the guards. They were still clinging to the tank ladder.

We can't stay out here all night. We'll freeze to death, Sato thought.

Below him, muddy water extended as far as he could see, its current growing stronger as time passed. He couldn't imagine how they could possibly get down.

Instead, he turned his eyes upward. About six meters above ground was a spiderweb of pipes and their supporting framework. The fuel, water, and high-voltage cables used at the factory traversed a network of pipes that was elevated for easy access, rather than being buried underground.

The support framework looked flimsy and dangerous. It wasn't built to be walked on, and if the power was still on a short somewhere could mean electrocution.

Sato looked down again.

But if we jump into that, we're dead for sure, he thought.

He could feel himself growing colder and weaker. Crossing to safety via the pipes was their only chance for survival. Sato mentally mapped out a route that would take them from building to building without needing to touch ground.

That he could do such a thing was another of the many small miracles that day. The plant grounds were something of a maze, and most workers only knew their way around the areas where they worked. Very few had a grasp of the overall layout. Sato knew every inch of the factory because he periodically performed fire inspections.

He called out to the guards.

"If we crawl across those supports, we can make it to the recycled pulp building. Let's move there."

"Got it," a guard shouted back.

The building they were heading for was twenty or thirty meters from the silo. Sato had hoped everyone could make it across, but the young nuclear plant worker was no longer able to walk. His leg seemed to be broken.

"You wait here," Sato told him. "Don't worry, we'll send someone back to help you."

One of the guards volunteered to stay behind with the young man.

Sato climbed to the top of the silo and jumped onto the framework. The support beam he needed to cross was only about fifty centimeters wide and covered in a thin layer of snow and ice. Below, the water swirled in eddies between the buildings. Sato looked at the beam in front of him. It was eaten through with corrosion in places, and he knew that if he stepped on the wrong spot, his foot would go straight through.

He edged forward. Although he was wearing work boots, his foot kept slipping out from beneath him. It was all he could do to keep his balance as he crossed, trying to step only on reinforced joints, which seemed the most likely to support his weight.

He heard a crashing sound and looked down to see the roof of a house below him. Glancing back, he saw that the guards were following him across the beam.

They finally reached the building. Sato tried the knob on the door that led to the roof and found it unlocked. They headed inside.

It was a sturdy concrete building. The silence inside made what was happening outside seem all the more unreal. Within the building everything remained as it had been before the tsunami hit. Outside, nothing was the same.

In an office, the group found pairs of chest-high rubber waders and a stretcher. Sato and one of the guards pulled on the waders. They picked up the stretcher and headed back outside through the ground-floor door.

They splashed through the water to the silo where the injured man was waiting, loaded him onto the stretcher, and headed back, struggling under his weight. Snow collected on Sato's eyebrows and eyelashes, obscuring his vision. When he shook the snow off he saw someone else calling for help in the distance, too far away to rescue.

Back in the recycled pulp building, Sato and the guard carried the man to the office and gently set him down. He was barely conscious.

"I guess we're stuck here until help arrives," Sato said.

"That'll be overnight at least."

"This building hasn't been used much recently, but there might be something to eat over in the groundwood pulp building. The third-shift folks keep food there for midnight snacks. People were probably working in there when the earthquake hit, so it might even be warm. There might be hot water too."

The others nodded and zipped their coats up more snugly. When they went back outside onto the roof, it felt even colder than before. They crossed another bridge between buildings, two of them bearing the young nuclear plant worker on the stretcher between them. They were high enough off the ground to feel dizzy each time they glanced down.

Entering the break room in the groundwood pulp building was like traveling back in time to the 1960s. Inside stood an ancient cupboard filled with dingy glasses, a brown vinyl sofa, a long, cheap-looking table, and little else. Although the lights were out, a faint warmth still lingered. It felt like heaven after the blustery cold outside. Shabby as it was, that room likely saved their lives.

In a locker room next door, they found some pink and brown blankets that employees used when napping. They tended to the injured man's wounds the best they could using a first-aid kit they had found, then wrapped him in blankets to try to warm him up.

Having secured a place to spend the night, Sato and the guards once again headed back out into the cold, taking with them a rope ladder they had found in an emergency stockpile. When they opened the steel door to the roof an icy wind hit them. They could hear people calling for help.

"I'm over here!"

"Help me, please!"

One was looking directly at Sato and waving.

"Over there," a guard said.

He pointed down to a young woman on top of a nearby garage, waving frantically.

"Hold on, we're coming," he shouted.

They moved as close to her as they could, secured the rope ladder, and tossed it down. After several attempts she caught hold of it. As she began climbing it sagged, lowering her into the water, but she managed to pull herself up. When she had climbed close enough, Sato reached out a hand and pulled her onto the roof. She appeared to be in her twenties.

"Let's get you inside," Sato said, leading the soaking wet woman to the break room. He found her a change of clothes and some blankets, then headed back out.

He could see three people stranded in the parking lot near the guard station, and five or six more farther away, south of the parking lot and water storage tanks. All were too far to reach.

"I wish there was something we could do, but..." Sato said despondently.

It was rapidly growing dark, so the group gave up and headed back to the break room.

Sato found some instant coffee, which he poured into cups and mixed with some warm water he found in a pot. He passed the coffee around, then drank his own. It was lukewarm but welcome nonetheless. Sato's slowly warming body was confirmation that he had survived.

Night came quickly. No lights illuminated the darkness outside. Sato turned on his flashlight, thankful for the fresh batteries, and everyone gathered around it. Outside they could hear wailing car alarms and horns.

They changed into work clothes they found in the locker room, wrapped themselves in blankets and squeezed together on the sofa to keep warm. For a long time everyone was silent.

After a while the woman they had saved related her experience.

"I was in my car on the road outside the factory when the tsunami suddenly carried me away. My car sank to the bottom and I started to get out, but when I looked up I could see all this debris flowing by so fast. I figured it would be dangerous to swim up through all that, so I waited there under water until it looked like I could make a break for it. When I got to the surface I climbed up on top of the garage."

"It's amazing that you kept your cool," somebody said.

Another long silence followed. A car alarm that had been sounding constantly nearby finally went quiet. Gradually the other alarms and horns faded away too, like living things dying one by one. In the silence Sato could still hear the shouts of those he had been unable to save echoing in his mind. He wrapped his blanket more tightly around himself and clutched his cell phone. The thought that stayed with him through the night was not *I don't want to die*, but rather *I can't die*. He would not let himself die before seeing his family again.

After many sleepless hours, he looked at the display on his cell phone. It read 4:00 AM. He tried calling his wife for the hundredth time and was surprised when he heard ring tones. The phone clicked and the call connected. His wife answered.

"Hey, it's me," he said. "Is everyone okay?"

"We are. We're okay."

"I am too. Alive, at least."

"We're afraid of aftershocks, so we're spending the night in the car."

"Good. I'll get home as soon as I can."

He briefly said a few more words and hung up. A bitter taste rose in his throat. The more the realization of his own survival settled in his mind, the more painful the memory of the faces of those left outside became. He was unable to sleep all night.

When dawn broke, Sato and the guards headed out again to see if they could find any survivors.

Sato stuck a chocolate bar he had found in the office into his pocket and scooped up an armful of blankets and plastic sheeting. Outside, the head guard gathered some scattered pallets and used them to create a makeshift bridge. Three people had taken refuge on top of a water supply pump nearby and were stranded there. Sato and the guards managed to crawl across the pallets to them.

One of the three, an elderly woman, had already died. The other two were too weak to move.

"Somebody will be along to help soon. Hang in there. Don't give up now."

Sato wrapped them in double layers of blankets and plastic sheeting. He pulled the chocolate bar out of his pocket and put it in the hand of one of the survivors.

They continued on to try to help another survivor. On the way they came across a group of five NPI employees who had formed a search party.

"We're so glad to see you!" one of them said. "We've cleared a path, over that way. Follow that and you can get out."

Later that morning they were in the emergency headquarters on Mt. Hiyori, where Murakami and the others were waiting.

Two more days passed before Sato was able to make his way home. His house was on high ground, untouched by the tsunami. When he arrived in his neighborhood everything looked just as it had before the earthquake hit. It was as if he had returned to a different world.

Electric, gas, and water services were still out, however, so the schools were closed and the streets were full of laughing, playing children. But seeing them brought Sato no happiness; it only confirmed to him the arbitrariness of natural disasters.

When he passed through the gate in front of his house, he saw his children cooking rice on a portable grill.

"It's Daddy! Daddy's home!" they shouted.

"I am," he said. "I'm home."

* * *

The actions of Murakami, Sato, and the NPI guards saved many lives that day—and possibly even the company itself. One reason they were able to lead the evacuation so skillfully was the company's commitment to safety training that valued saving lives above all else. Employees had begun large-scale evacuation drills after the Chilean earthquake, and procedures were improved through employee feedback after each trial. Had the evacuation been less smooth, the company could have lost many skilled workers. Upper management would have been blamed for those losses, leading to serious repercussions for the company as a whole. At a minimum, employees would have lost faith in NPI. That did not happen.

Nonetheless, things could have been done better, as a number of employees pointed out.

"We were lucky, when it comes right down to it," Sato says. "It's truly a miracle that everyone managed to evacuate that day. For one thing it took a long time for the tsunami to arrive after the earthquake, but had it hit closer we might have had just five minutes before it hit. If that'd been the case for us, then considering how slowly everyone was moving we'd have been too late. So we recently changed our plan. If a large earthquake hits, we won't be evacuating to Mt. Hiyori, but rather to the second floor or higher of the nearest sturdy building. Someplace like the main machine building, which is made of reinforced concrete and is box-shaped. So long as we're careful of things falling from overhead, that's by far the safest place to be."

I asked how he felt when he heard that everyone had evacuated safely.

"Relieved, of course. But remember that when they say 'everyone,' they mean everyone who was on duty. We lost coworkers who were off work that day, so it's hard to feel completely happy. I work in human resources, and I help with pensions and severance pay. For over four months after the earthquake I was assisting the spouses and parents of employees who lost their lives in the disaster. Having experienced the tsunami myself made it even harder."

Sato fell silent for a while, and when he spoke again his words came with more difficulty.

"I can't shake the feeling that if I'd tried harder I could've saved more people. Honestly, I wish I could forget the whole thing."

He closed our interview with this:

"And the ocean... I can't even look at it anymore, much less enjoy it. As close as it is, I haven't looked at it once since that day."

*Logs and woodchips scattered
during the disaster*

CHAPTER 3

Decisions

1

Paper mills produce a variety of paper products using a range of manufacturing processes. At the Ishinomaki plant, the process begins with extracting pulp, or wood fiber, the main raw material for paper. The three main kinds of pulp used in paper are recycled pulp, chemical pulp, and mechanical pulp.

Recycled pulp is obtained by using water and chemicals to dissolve old newspapers and other recyclable paper products to extract the wood fibers. Newsprint typically contains about 80 % recycled pulp.

Chemical pulp is created by boiling woodchips in caustic soda in a vessel called a digester, then extracting the fibers. Pulp extracted in this way produces strong, smooth paper. Most high-quality paper is produced using chemical pulp.

There are several methods for producing mechanical pulp. In one, wood chips are ground down in a machine called a refiner, screened to remove dust, then bleached. Paper made from mechanical pulp absorbs ink very well and has a high opacity, meaning that print on one side does not show through on the other. It also has high bulk, or cushioning, making it soft. This type of paper is ideal for printing comics.

Pulp mixtures are pounded and pressed to cause the fibers within to blend and tangle, then fed into a machine that turns them into paper.

Manufacturing processes vary for different types of paper. For coated paper, the most common type, the process begins by diluting pulp with water into a slurry. The slurry is sprayed over a fine wire mesh to separate out most of the water, leaving behind a thin sheet of wet fibers. This sheet passes between felt-lined rollers, which absorb most of the remaining water. The paper is then fully dried by pressing it against cylinders that are heated from within using steam.

The dried paper passes through a coater, which applies a very thin layer of powdered materials such as coal and clay. This coating allows ink to better adhere to the paper and gives it the desired sheen. Finally, the paper passes through a machine called a calender, which presses it between a series of rollers to polish it and remove irregularities.

The completed paper then leaves the machine and is rolled onto enormous "jumbo reels," then onto smaller reels via a machine called a winder. These smaller reels are separated using a cutter, processed into sheets or spools, and delivered to customers.

The feel of paper is largely determined by the blend of fibers used to produce it. This is an important consideration, because one of the most attractive features of paper books is the texture of their pages. Pulps created from conifer trees, broadleaf trees, groundwood (untreated pulp generally used for newsprint), and recycled paper each contain fibers with differing softness. By blending these pulps, the paper maker is able to tailor the product to its intended use.

In recent years the media world has exploded with new formats: television, portable music players, smart phones, personal computers, video games, and more. These formats stimulate our eyes and ears, yet neglect our sense of touch and smell—two of the key senses activated when we read a paper book. I believe these sensory experiences play an important role in helping us to better understand and remember what we read.

No doubt many readers recall the experience of purchasing a new book they'd been looking forward to—the happiness evoked by the smell of the freshly printed pages and the feel of their crisp, unbent surface. With a paper book, the reading experience begins before we even open the cover, and when we begin to turn the pages texture and scent alter our experience of the world within.

As we sink deeper into this experience, we add traces of our passage. We turn down corners to mark spots we deem significant. We crease the book's spine over the course of many visits to a favorite page, so that it falls open as if by magic to that very place. We leave tears on the scenes that make us cry and stains from spilled coffee on pages that make us laugh. Crayon scribbles remind us of our favorite childhood picture books, while tickets and postcards used as bookmarks sleep like fond memories between pages, waiting to be found again.

Although we are rarely conscious of these small experiences, they deepen our understanding of a book's content and leave it more firmly embedded in our memory.

As I mentioned above, there are many types of paper, each suited to its intended use. The paper used in dictionaries, for instance, is very thin, yet sturdy enough to withstand constant handling. It must also resist the buildup of static electricity, and therefore requires a high level of technical skill to produce.

The paper used in magazines should contribute to a fun, engaging reading experience. Recently, magazine companies have favored thick, soft papers that send readers a subliminal message of luxury and enjoyment as they turn each page. Often a single magazine contains several types of paper. These pages of contrasting texture are called accent pages, signaling to the reader that a new section is beginning. They are also designed to hold the reader's interest; if every page feels the same, boredom ensues. Flipping through accent pages sends a new signal from the fingertips to the brain, stimulating curiosity toward the unknown.

Literary books require a different kind of matchmaking between paper and content. Bookbinders and editors first read the manuscript, then choose an appropriate surface to print it on. The paper, as well as the cover materials they eventually settle on, plays a large role in determining the impression readers will form of the book. The task is a delicate one—simply using a high-quality paper will not ensure a high-quality book, and using a whiter paper does not guarantee it will feel bright and fresh. Texture and gloss also contribute to a book's personality, conveying its worldview and deepening its impact on the reader.

Editors dedicated to making the most beautiful book possible sometimes visit paper mills in pursuit of a specific vision. For instance, bulkier paper can feel luxurious, but too much bulk makes paper overly stiff, and that leads to pages that won't beautifully overlap when the book is open. An editor printing the Bible once gave NPI the following instructions: "I need a book that opens in the shape of an ox's horn and has the graceful curve of a drawn bow."

Mr. Hatanaka, a technician at NPI's Ishinomaki plant, has run countless trials in his attempts to create paper that meets the conflicting needs for high bulk and softness. His job is a difficult one because customers tend to order in sensory terms. "We need something with a graceful feel," they'll say, leaving him to figure out exactly what it means for paper to feel "graceful" and how to manufacture it.

Trends in preferences for paper gloss and color shift over the years. Shun Kato, an employee at NPI's Tokyo sales division when the earthquake hit, told me about the kind of paper that was popular in years before.

"There was a time when our customers thought the glossier a paper was, the better. But recently they've started to think that overly shiny paper looks tawdry, and now everyone wants a more natural sheen and texture. With the exception of special-use metallics, most of what we produce now is natural-feeling paper. There are also trends in colors. Most book pages used to be cream-colored, but in the past few years whites and super-whites have become more popular. Maybe it's a reflection of the desire to make this a brighter era."

Noriaki Sato, the leader of Machine 8, also spoke about paper color.

"A few years back, everybody wanted bluish paper for textbooks. The trend apparently started in Europe. But lighting is different in Europe, and Japanese and Europeans have different tastes, so recently everyone here is going back to more natural hues."

All paper companies maintain closely guarded "secret recipes." The methods and chemicals used for finishing are the result of many years of research and are passed on within factories as important intellectual property. But as with food, a good recipe is not enough—just as it takes a master chef to turn a recipe into the perfect meal, it takes skilled technicians performing careful, delicate adjustments to the manufacturing process to produce excellent paper.

As NPI's main source of paper for the printing industry, the Ishinomaki plant was without question the heart of the company. However, demand for paper in Japan had been falling in the years before the disaster as new digital media tools took off and the population aged. The printing industry in particular was feeling the pain. Employees of the Ishinomaki plant knew this, and the same question burned in everyone's mind:

Would NPI rebuild the plant, or would they shut it down?

2

On the day of the earthquake, employees in the sales division at NPI's Tokyo headquarters worked through the night trying to determine the situation at the plant so they could inform newspaper and publishing companies as to when and how their orders would be filled.

They learned that 36,000 tons of product had been awaiting shipment at the Ishinomaki mill when the disaster hit and that Machine 8 had been manufacturing paper for Kadokawa Publishing at the time. Another 30,000 tons of product was ready for shipment at the Iwanuma mill in southern Miyagi prefecture. Some inventory was also stored at a warehouse in Tokyo, but the building's automated lifts had collapsed in the earthquake, making it impossible to ship product.

As the president of NPI, Yoshio Haga's top priority was figuring out how to provide his customers with the paper they needed in order to continue printing without interruption. The Iwanuma mill, located just south of Sendai, was the main supplier of paper for newspapers in the Tohoku region. Haga needed to quickly assess the damage to factories outside the region and determine whether they could make up the lost production capacity—and if so, when they could deliver.

Haga knew he was on thin ice; if he lost the Ishinomaki mill, the rest of NPI could go down with it. At the time, the company had 3,884 employees throughout the country. Counting employees at affiliated companies brought the total to 13,834. His decisions over the next few days would have a huge impact on the fate of those individuals and even on the city of Ishinomaki.

By the following morning, directors and department chiefs at the Tokyo office had formed an emergency response team, with Haga as its head. He spent the day visiting the Ministry of Economy, Trade, and Industry and delivering status reports on the company to government representatives from Miyagi and other prefectures. He also dispatched employees to newspapers and printers to do the same.

By March 13, a clearer picture of the situation in Ishinomaki was finally beginning to emerge, and the company's priority shifted to delivering food, water, and fuel to the disaster area. Haga declared a state of emergency, and delivered the following message to his employees:

As we learn more, it has become increasingly clear that this is the largest natural disaster in recent history. The scale of the destruction is greater than anything we had ever imagined. The tsunami in particular has caused massive damage. Confirming the status of the Ishinomaki mill is currently a top priority. Roads and other vital infrastructure have been destroyed, and recovery will likely be an extremely long, difficult process.

This disaster represents the greatest danger this company has ever faced. We must do everything we can to support our fellow workers in the disaster area, repair the damage, and restore production. Our tasks are to swiftly calculate the impact of this event on our company and to overcome the many obstacles we will likely face in the coming days in order to rebuild it.

In the days following the disaster Haga was also receiving reports of the destruction to other parts of Ishinomaki. An elementary school had caught fire and burned to the ground. Fires at the base of Mt. Hiyori were enveloping the hill in smoke. Rumors circulated that the NPI factory was likely destroyed.

No one at the company was so optimistic as to think that the Ishinomaki mill would be functioning again anytime soon. Many thought it would have to be shut down permanently, and even the most optimistic assumed recovery would require several years.

But Haga told me the idea of closing down the mill never crossed his mind.

"I never even considered it at the time," he said. "It was far too early to make decisions like that. Before we decided anything, we had to wait for the waters to recede so we could get a clearer picture of the damage. I wanted to see the situation with my own eyes before deciding anything."

But the mill was still buried under mountains of rubble that would prevent thorough investigation. "I'm ready to go any time," he told the factory manager. "Just let me know when it's possible." Haga knew he would soon need to make some quick decisions about the future of the company. But for now the disaster area was such a shambles that supplies could not even be delivered, and his employees were starving. For the time being, his main priority was making sure they received the goods they needed to survive.

3

Ishinomaki is a city blessed with a bountiful water supply, but after the disaster water turned into a major obstacle.

The tsunami had flooded everything along the coastline. It had traveled up the Kitakami River, which snakes from the east side of Mt. Hiyori to its north, and deposited barricades of automobiles and wrecked houses on bridges. The tsunami had also flooded canals to the west of the mill, leaving it surrounded by water on all four sides. No one knew when the waters would recede.

By the second day following the earthquake, the NPI employees stranded on Mt. Hiyori were becoming desperate for food. Managers scrounged for rice in the company dormitories and cooked it for the employees. The rice balls were tiny and had no seasoning or filling, but to the starving survivors they were a welcome feast. Several employees told me they had never eaten anything so delicious, and that they were so thankful they cried.

Murakami discussed the situation with his fellow managers. "We can't survive like this much longer. We need to tell headquarters to charter a helicopter and bring us some food."

He never would have considered making such a request under normal circumstances, and he had no idea what the cost would be, but the food situation was becoming desperate.

Murakami was still wearing the suit he'd worn to his meeting at city hall, with no coat to buffer the cold. He had wrung out as much water as possible from his clothes, however, and thankfully they had finally dried.

He found the satellite phone and called company headquarters.

"We need you to charter a helicopter," he said. "We need you to deliver enough food for 1,000 people to live off of for three days."

At the baseball field on the hill he found a machine for marking off white lines and used it to draw a large H to indicate where the helicopter should land. In the end it wasn't needed, as supplies soon arrived by truck. But Murakami's impromptu landing field did see use by rescue helicopters from the fire department.

The first supplies reached the NPI employees on the morning of March 14, from an affiliated company in Kyoto. The Hanshin earthquake of 1995 was still a fresh memory for people in that part of Japan, and they immediately understood the seriousness of the situation. They had loaded emergency supplies onto trucks and dispatched them even before receiving any requests for aid. The drivers took shifts so that they wouldn't have to stop. With so many roads impassable due to earthquake damage, the drivers had to look for alternate routes, stretching what should have been a ten-hour drive to three days. Finally, however, the trucks reached Ishinomaki.

When they arrived and began unloading, the NPI employees were so relieved that many began to cry. They hadn't been abandoned after all. Later that day more trucks began arriving from other NPI factories and affiliated companies.

Bags of supplies from NPI's factory in Kumamoto prefecture carried handwritten messages: "You guys hang in there!" and "You are stronger than the earthquake!"

As their relief subsided, however, the employees realized that many of the evacuation sites nearby were still waiting for food and other supplies. They decided to take some of what they had received to the city hall for redistribution. Residents in the area had done plenty to help NPI employees; now it was their turn to give something back.

There was not enough to supply all the evacuation sites, however. At the evacuation sites near the company housing, many people were still receiving only half a banana as a meal ration. Some began to feel resentful, and rumors spread that NPI was taking an unfair share of the supplies.

Other tensions simmered as well. NPI allowed employees who had lost their homes to move into unused company-owned houses, and while those who were able to get in were thankful, two or three families were sharing each house. Stresses piled up.

Security began to deteriorate, too. Some people tried to steal bicycles from the dormitory parking lots, and others tried to siphon gasoline from the tanks of parked cars. To prevent this, employees began parking their cars so closely together that the fuel caps couldn't be opened. Someone discovered a retired employee trying to take water from a storage tank. When confronted, he became angry and insisted he had a right to it. After that the NPI employees organized patrols to walk around the area in shifts.

On March 25 the company paid each employee a salary of ¥100,000 (around US$1,000) in cash. To do so, accounting manager Taniguchi had to carry a sack stuffed with over ¥10 million (US$100,000) from the bank. "Now that I think about it that was a dumb thing to do, given how dangerous things had become," he says.

It was also possibly a pointless thing to do—no stores were open in the area, so money was of little use.

4

Ishinomaki mill chief Hiromi Kurata was in a company Lexus in the vicinity of the Sendai train station, returning from the baseball tournament in Tokyo, when he felt the earth begin to shake violently.

Thankfully the tsunami did not reach him, but as he and his driver proceeded toward Ishinomaki they discovered that a wide area surrounding the factory was submerged and that all the roads to Mt.

Hiyori were blocked. They ended up stranded in a supermarket parking lot on the edge of the city. From its roof he could see black smoke rising from the direction of the factory. *It must be hell there*, he thought.

The following day he headed for the factory on foot, figuring that even if the water was waist deep he could still wade there. On the way he met a man coming from the opposite direction. He was wearing a wetsuit.

"What's it like back there?" Kurata asked.

"Up to here," the man said, holding a hand up to his throat.

Kurata gave up and turned back.

On March 13 he ran into an acquaintance, who told him it was possible to approach Mt. Hiyori by walking along the embankments lining the Kitagawa River. Kurata headed off toward the factory once again.

The wind was strong that day. Many other people were walking listlessly along the embankments, but no one spoke, and they all looked exhausted. They reminded Kurata of war refugees fleeing their burned-out homes.

When he entered the city through Sumiyoshi Park, he saw several large boats lying across the road. Traffic signals and utility poles were snapped in two, and cars dangled from trees and buildings. When he finally got a view from the top of Mt. Hiyori, the destroyed city below him looked gray and dead. He could see the factory from where he was. The smokestacks were still standing, but no steam issued from them.

The factory is dead, he thought.

Kurata had been assigned to the Ishinomaki mill eight months earlier. NPI was formed through a series of corporate mergers, so many high-level managers came from previously independent companies. Even so, Kurata had a unique background.

After graduating from Kogakuin University in 1970, he was hired at the Kokusaku Pulp Mill, which would eventually merge with NPI. He worked there for four years as a paper machine operator at their Asahikawa mill. It was unusual for college graduate career-track hires to work a shift job for so long. Those destined for management generally spent their days doing deskwork and climbing the corporate ladder. But immediately after Kurata was hired his supervisor had sent him to a factory, saying he looked strong enough for real work.

The idea behind putting college graduates to work on the factory floor was that they would get to know the business better, but they were often unpopular with the permanent shift workers. Higher-ups would soon receive complaints that the management-track workers were clumsy and useless and ought to be sent back to an office. Some of those assigned to jobs on the floor quit in indignation. As a result, the company pulled back on the policy, and most of its management-track employees had never experienced shift work.

Kurata thrived on it, however. The division he was assigned to ran a machine that produced newsprint. He worked day, evening, and night shifts—an irregular rhythm that required a certain physical and mental toughness. Ishinomaki's cutting-edge Number 6 paper machine is a slim, stylish apparatus whose inner workings are hidden by silver paneling. In contrast, the Number 1 machine Kurata operated at Kokusaku was a hulking thing with exposed innards. If the Number 6 machine was a jumbo jet, the Number 1 machine was a propeller airplane. A tough one, though; it is still in service today.

"Honestly, four years in the factory is only enough to learn the very basics," Kurata says. "But those four years served me well in everything I did after that." His intuitive feel for what happens on the factory floor became an important management skill.

Another of his strengths came from the fact that he had helped restructure several factories in Hokkaido. He knew well the strengths of a factory crew and just when to complain about things. Factory workers would often complain to their higher-ups. Some were just grumbling, but others were raising valid issues that needed to be addressed. Kurata had the skill and experience to distinguish between the two.

He also knew that when his workers promised to knuckle down and get a job done, they would do what it took, no matter what obstacles they encountered. Dealing with the unexpected was a daily occurrence for them; half the problems they dealt with had no solutions laid out in troubleshooting manuals. More than anything else, Kurata knew how strongly his workers could push back when they were forced into a corner.

Experiencing a natural disaster can feel like being struck by the hand of God. The mill was facing a danger unlike anything it had experienced before. It was therefore a lucky stroke of fate that the workers there had a leader who knew exactly what they were capable of achieving.

On March 14 Kurata finally reached the mill and along with a group of workers, entered it for the first time since the earthquake.

The waves had washed so much debris up against the front gates that at first it seemed impossible to enter. Kurata found a gap in the fence, however, and peered in at the factory he was responsible for.

What he saw amazed him: The second floors of houses. Shipping containers and small trucks haphazardly tossed about. One-ton bales of paper for recycling scattered like toys. Trucks dangling from the sides of buildings against which they had been hurled with such force that they had pierced the walls.

Kurata had seen photos of the tsunami's aftermath, and he thought he was prepared for what he would encounter. But seeing the wreckage with his own eyes was entirely different. He had never been in the factory when machines weren't running, and the silence was disconcerting. The only sound was the squishing of their galoshes as the group trudged through the mud.

Kurata looked up at the smokestacks. He had never seen them without billowing clouds of steam. The snow clouds had passed, leaving behind a brilliantly blue sky. "It was such a beautiful day," he recalls.

Accompanying Kurata that day was Toru Ikeuchi, who was in charge of maintaining the mill's electrical system.

"It was just awful," he says. "I didn't think there was any way we could recover. I didn't even know where we would begin to try. There were nearly 11,000 motors in the factory, and of those around 7,000 had been submerged in muddy water. Everything on the first floor of the buildings was ruined. Only machines located on upper floors could be salvaged."

As everyone knows, water is the enemy of electricity. Now Ikeuchi was faced with a capillary-like network of electrical equipment and wiring that had been soaked in mud and saltwater.

There was no trace of the 66,000-volt line that had previously encircled the factory. It was like a living creature with a major artery ripped out. Who would believe that such a thing could be brought back to life? Ikeuchi began to mentally prepare himself for the plant being shut down.

As Ikeuchi stood there, grimly realizing it would probably be easier to build a new factory than to repair this one, Kurata had a dizzy spell and collapsed to the ground. Ikeuchi and the others helped him back up and supported him as they turned and left the factory grounds.

5

Ishinomaki plant managers held daily meetings at the NPI clubhouse on Mt. Hiyori. Now that they had food, their top priority was helping everyone get back to something resembling their previous lives.

By March 17 they had secured a diesel generator to power company houses, but they only had enough fuel to run it a few hours each day. They held many of their meetings by candlelight.

Prior to the tsunami, the company had prepared an organizational chart for setting up an emergency response team in the event of a disaster, but just a glance was enough to tell the managers that it wouldn't be of much use. They used construction paper and markers to make their own list of the teams they would need to form: toilet management, garbage incineration, communications, confirmation of the safety of off-duty employees, neighborhood patrol, relief goods distribution… The list made them all the more aware of how far away "everyday life" really was.

Toilets were a particularly pressing concern. The management group had issued a warning that with no water toilets in homes would not work and shouldn't be used. The company houses had septic tanks, but since they weren't running they might overflow if used. If that happened they wouldn't function even when the power and water were restored, and it would take days to get them repaired. With no other option available, they decided to dig a latrine in the empty space between the houses.

Kazuhiro Nakata of the administration division gathered some of the stronger young men to tackle this task. He asked one of them, a man named Shimura from the R&D division, to head up the team.

"I had mixed feelings about the assignment, but Mr. Nakata was head of the committee that hired me, so I couldn't say no," he laughs. "I'd been hoping for a leadership position someday, but Chief of Toilets wasn't exactly what I had in mind."

Shimura didn't have time to bemoan his new job, however. It was an important task, and he set to it immediately.

Many of the other survivors were also experiencing conflicting emotions. Even those whose homes and families were safe were surrounded by colleagues and friends suffering immense losses. The joy of pulling through unharmed was tinged with gratitude and guilt. But few complained. Those who were able to work pitched in where they could. Working felt better than sitting around thinking about the situation.

Between ten and twenty young employees from NPI and its affiliated companies joined the toilet task force. They gathered what shovels they could find and began digging away at the frozen earth, creating a hole to use as a latrine. It was still cold, with lows below zero and highs of 6 to 7 °C at best, and their breath made white clouds as they worked. The ground was harder than they expected. Every layer of earth they dug through uncovered a more tightly packed stratum beneath.

They dug as deep as they could, knowing that a too-shallow latrine would soon fill up. Even working in ten-minute shifts, the cold and unfamiliar labor made for difficult going. Still, no one complained, and the group continued digging in silence.

The job took half a day. When they finished digging they placed metal grating on either side of the hole for users to stand on.

"Good job," Shimura said. "I wonder if we can't find something to cover it up with."

In a storage area, one of the crew found a white tent used for school activities. They erected it over the hole, completing their makeshift toilet.

Their most immediate problem was now solved, but another arose after a few days of use. Everyone had assumed that urine would naturally soak into the earth, but instead it pooled in the packed dirt. Despite the cold, the area was soon enveloped in the pungent stench of ammonia. Over 100 people were living in the company housing, so it wouldn't take long for any hand-dug hole to fill to overflowing.

The situation worsened when rain came, and Shimura grew worried. He wasn't surprised when Nakata asked him to do something about the problem.

He and his team walked to the latrine. When they arrived, they saw that it was already almost full. Rain was dripping in, making ripples in the murky yellowish pool. The team members looked at each other.

"Anybody got any ideas?"

They tried filling the hole back in, but shoveling in dirt cast a spray about their feet, and the earth just displaced equal amounts of sewage, making an overflow a certainty.

"I don't think we can do anything about this one," Shimura said. "We'll just have to dig another."

Shimura had heard on the news about the sanitation problems victims of the 1995 Kobe earthquake had experienced. Back then it had seemed like a remote issue. *And now here I am in the same situation*, he thought. He found it odd that despite all he'd seen in the actual earthquake and tsunami, he'd never felt so much like a refugee as when he stood there staring at the pool of sewage.

They began digging a new hole near the first one. As the work went on, they became increasingly wet and muddy. The job grew colder and harder with each shovelful of dirt.

A few days later a health worker came by and asked what they were using for a toilet. When an NPI employee took her to their latrine, she was shocked.

"You can't use this!" she said.

"Nothing else to use," he replied.

She promised to have portable toilets delivered and to arrange for a sanitation truck to come by daily to empty them. They finally arrived on March 21.

Water service to the area wouldn't be restored until April 6. Unable to bathe, many male employees began shaving their heads.

As the days grew warmer, flies infested the area. They were everywhere, but in some places they formed black swarms so dense they made ordinary objects look like the corpse of some dead animal.

Warmer weather also brought with it a powerful stench—Ishinomaki is a fishing town, and the massive quantities of fish stored in broken freezers throughout the waterfront district had begun to rot. Huge flocks of seagulls feasted on the fish, staining their beaks a disgusting ochre color.

Soon after the earthquake, NPI's Tokyo headquarters began receiving a deluge of relief supplies from clients and from its own factories located outside the Tohoku region. Employees loaded these donations onto four-ton trucks, sending one off almost every day. Publishers like Shueisha and Shogakukan also donated stacks of comics for children in the disaster area.

Akira Kanamori, technical division director at the Ishinomaki mill, recalls the comic deliveries with a laugh. "The shrewd kids around here saw their chance and started putting in requests."

The large publishing house Kodansha dispatched a storytelling brigade to Ishinomaki, delighting local children and helping them get through the most difficult period. The company sent books for adults too. Among them was an anthology by 98-year old poet Toyo Shibata titled *Kujikenaide*, or "Don't Lose Heart."

6

Small regional cities don't offer much of a nightlife, so the most common form of stress relief for division managers at the Ishinomaki factory was getting together for drinks at a local pub. When that closed, they would continue drinking in the dormitories reserved for single men. Normally much of their talk would be good-natured bickering about whose section was most responsible for cost overruns. The closeness they formed in these gripe sessions proved beneficial during the disaster.

One night in late March the same group of managers gathered in a dorm room to hold an emergency response committee meeting. The building was an old concrete apartment whose entryway led directly to a small combined living and dining room, with a tatami-floored room next to that. The group was sitting on the floor around a low table.

Among them that night was the mill chief Kurata. He is a soft-spoken man, but exudes the air of someone whose judgment is not to be questioned. He began speaking to the section managers about the factory's future.

"Everybody is exhausted and worried about what's going to happen. We need some kind of specific goal, something to motivate them."

The other managers listened with interest. They weren't sure what upper management in Tokyo had in mind, but it sounded like Kurata was talking about getting the plant open and running again.

As Kurata had said, it was stressful to watch the days pass by without knowing whether or not the mill would reopen. The immense scale of destruction in town brought on a sense of crushing despair. Most of the employees seemed to be toughing it out so far, but the managers knew human resolve had its limits—it wouldn't be long before sadness and depression took over. They shared Kurata's sense that rather than sitting around waiting, they should take it on faith that NPI wouldn't give up on Ishinomaki. They needed to establish some goal that everyone could work toward.

"I think the first thing to do is to set a deadline for recovery," Kurata continued. "We don't have to bring all the machines back online, but at least one. That would be enough to show the world that we are recovering, which would be a big morale boost for our employees."

Those around him nodded in agreement. Getting one machine up and running seemed like a reasonable goal and would be a clear indication that they were getting back on their feet. But Kurata's next words shocked them.

"Half a year," he said. "That has to be our deadline. Six months."

No one dared speak against him, but Kanamori felt ready to scream. *Six months!? The old man is insane…*

They all had seen the devastation in the town below. Heaps of debris and pools of dirty water were everywhere. The mill was such a shambles that it was hard to even tell where it began or ended. The thought of cleaning everything up and getting a machine back online in six months seemed too optimistic to even dream about.

"This was the head of the entire factory we were talking to," Kanamori says, "practically a god from our point of view. But six months? We didn't even have electricity. We hadn't even been able to get deep enough inside the mill to fully survey the damage. There was no way he had any idea how much this would cost or how long it would take. What we did know was that he was asking the impossible. All of the plant managers agreed. With all due respect, at the time we thought the guy was crazy."

Kurata's approach was the opposite of what they had been trained to do. In engineering, timelines are established by starting from the first processes, figuring out what it will take to complete them, then adding new processes in turn until the goal is reached. They needed to know how long it would take to get electricity running, how long to repair the water system, how long to get the boilers operational again… It was supposed to be an additive process, but this time the final completion date was being set first; deadlines for all the necessary subtasks would have to follow suit. To get a machine running by this day its digester would have to be operational by that day, and so on all the way back. The deadlines for the electrical and mechanical divisions would be too unrealistic to even consider.

"It just isn't possible. That's what I thought at first," Tamai from the motives division told me. "Even if you give me a deadline, I can't make any progress toward it without water. Without electricity, there's no water. The more I thought about it, the more insane it seemed. We hadn't even started yet and we were already behind schedule. The whole thing was just laughable."

Ikeuchi from the electrical division summed up his opinion more succinctly:

"No way. Just...no way."

Pushing back against superiors goes against the norms of Japanese business culture, so the group of managers present that night didn't express their true feelings to Kurata. Yet they all shared a single thought: *Let him build castles in the sky. Let him set some ridiculous goal and watch as one division or another fails to meet it. Eventually he'll realize he's asking the impossible and revise the timeline. Just please don't let it be my team that falls behind and gets blamed for throwing everything off schedule. Let it be somebody else.*

But as Kurata continued to speak, his words became increasingly persuasive.

"Two years, even one year is too long. Anything longer than half a year is too distant to motivate everyone. Right now we're riding on our customers' sympathy, but that can only last so long. Business is business—they won't wait forever. Even a month is a pretty long time. Six months is pushing it. I'm just talking about one machine. We can do that."

Kanamori knew all too well that Kurata was right. Failure to move fast would doom the factory, which in turn might doom the entire company. The fate of NPI was on their shoulders. They had no other choice.

No matter how unreasonable Kurata's decision seemed, it was based on an understanding of worker psychology. He knew that if he assigned his employees the task of saving the company in six months, they would do everything in their power to meet that goal.

Later he said, "I knew from the beginning I was asking the impossible.

I wouldn't have been disappointed if they didn't succeed. But without a concrete goal, nobody would have known which way they should be heading."

When I mentioned his words to some of the section leaders, they all shook their heads.

"Regardless of what he says now, at the time we got the feeling that failure was not an option."

Kurata believed strong leadership would be a key to their success.

"Whether a team makes its goal or not depends on its leader," he later said. "If the leader says it will take two years, it will take two years. If the leader says three, then three. And if six months is the goal, then with good leadership the job will get done in six months. If we'd relied on common sense, even three years wouldn't have been enough."

"Recovery in six months!" became a rallying cry among the managers. Regardless of their doubts, they began to see it as a deadline for the survival of the company.

Yet one can't help wondering if that's all they felt. Given the gloomy environment of the disaster area, it's possible that this seemingly unattainable goal provided their only glimmer of hope. Their daily lives had been stolen from them, and something they needed in order to feel human again might possibly lie on the other side of that goal.

7

CEO Haga decided he couldn't wait any longer.

"I'm coming. I'll be in Ishinomaki on March 26," he declared.

He had been in contact with retired friends from the Ishinomaki mill, and they were sounding increasingly despondent.

"Rumor around here is that you're going to shut down the mill," one said. "Is that true?"

"Oh, come on. Does that really sound like something I would do?"

Haga didn't consider closing the plant an option. Even if the only thing salvaged was the new N6 machine, there was hope for recovery. But without the Ishinomaki plant NPI would collapse sooner or later. Haga knew recovery wouldn't be easy, but he was committed to it from the beginning—and one reason he needed to visit the factory as soon as possible was to reassure employees on the ground of that commitment.

Haga departed Tokyo with four other executives: emergency response committee leader Fujisaki, labor union head Miyazaki, chief secretary Iwamoto, and director of public relations Yoshino.

To be sure they wouldn't be a burden in the disaster area, they loaded a four-wheel-drive truck with all the food, cigarettes, alcohol, and extra tanks of gasoline it could hold. On the way they spent the night in neighboring Fukushima prefecture, then left for Ishinomaki at dawn.

They were able to take the expressway most of the way, but in Fukushima they began to notice undulations in the road—first-hand evidence of just how powerful the earthquake had been. Near Sendai the damage became so severe they were forced to switch to a local highway. They crossed the Naruse River and passed through the mountains, emerging at the Japan Self-Defense Force's Matsushima base. The Ishinomaki mill loomed on the horizon.

Haga had traveled the same route many times before, and the sight of the factory like a hulking battleship in the distance had always given him pleasure. The steam billowing from its smokestacks had been reassurance that the plant was humming along. But on March 26, the mill looked like a pale corpse under a thin shroud of snow.

When they got off the highway they began to see scattered piles of debris. A river embankment had collapsed, and in place of the houses that had once stood in the area, a lake now stretched all the way back to the Matsushima base. The first floors of the houses on the other side of the river had been washed out, leaving ragged frames to support the upper stories.

It was a heartbreaking sight, unlike anything the five men had ever seen. As the car crept forward, nosing around the wreckage strewn over the road, conversation trailed off. Haga sat silently, looking out the window.

In a sense, the Ishinomaki mill got its start as a way to support tsunami survivors.

The Tohoku region—including Ishinomaki—was ravaged first by the Showa financial crisis of the late 1920s and then by the Sanriku earthquake and tsunami of 1933. To promote economic revitalization, the government established a company called Tohoku Kogyo K. K. in 1936.

In 1940 that company, along with the Tohoku Pulp Company, opened a paper factory in Ishinomaki. The Tohoku Pulp Company had been established two years earlier by Oji Paper Company president Ginjiro Fujiwara (Japan's "Paper King") after Fujiwara took note of the region's bountiful beech forests.

In 1949 Tohoku Kogyo Pulp changed its name to Tohoku Pulp. In the same year Oji Paper Company was split up as a part of the US Occupation efforts toward zaibatsu dissolution, resulting in the formation of the Jujo Paper Company. Tohoku Pulp merged with Jujo Paper Company in 1968, creating the Jujo Paper Ishinomaki Paper Mill. As a result of a 1993 merger with Sanyo-Kokusaku Pulp the factory was renamed as the Nippon Paper Industries Ishinomaki Mill, which merged with Daishowa Paper Manufacturing Company in 2003.

Ishinomaki is well suited to the paper industry in several important ways. The Kitakami River supplies the bountiful clean water required by the manufacturing process, the vast forests of the Tohoku region supply the wood pulp used as a base material, and established transportation routes to Tokyo allow for efficient product delivery. For these reasons NPI invested heavily in the Ishinomaki plant as its core production facility.

Since the 1968 merger, the factory has added six paper machines, three coaters, two continuous digesters for dissolving wood chips, and four lines for processing recycled paper. In 2007 it acquired the N6 paper machine, an integrated "on-machine coater" that combines paper manufacturing and coating processes. The N in N6 stands for "new," to distinguish it as a next-generation machine fundamentally different from older devices, which were named in order as machines 1 through 10.

The device can produce over 1,000 tons of paper per day at a rate of 1,800 meters per minute. It is one of the largest, most advanced machines of its kind in the world, and building it cost NPI around ¥63 billion (approximately US$630 million). In comparison the total construction budget for the Tokyo Skytree—the tallest tower in the world—was around ¥65 billion.

While on-machine coaters in other countries are single units built by a single manufacturer, the N6 machine combines components from Voith in Germany, Metso Corporation in Finland, and Yodoko in Japan, taking advantage of each manufacturer's particular strengths.

With the completion of this machine, the Ishinomaki mill established itself as a globally competitive facility. The production volume of the N6 machine alone was extraordinary, dwarfing that of smaller paper mills. Equally important, the machine was operated by a team of highly skilled technicians capable of meeting the demands of any publishing company.

This is what the tsunami destroyed, and what Haga was determined to rebuild.

When the truck pulled up to the clubhouse, Haga was greeted by a waiting line of nervous employees. Among them, Haga found union leader Suzuki. Haga had once worked with Suzuki's father in Ishinomaki.

Haga approached Suzuki, took off his glove, and gave him a firm handshake.

"Is your dad okay?" Haga asked.

"He is, thank you."

"I'm glad to hear that." Haga smiled warmly at Suzuki. "Don't you worry about the factory now."

On hearing those reassuring words, a tear spilled from Suzuki's eye. *He's going to reopen the plant*, Suzuki thought. *He's going to save the jobs of 600 employees.*

Suzuki was head of the factory's labor union. He had been listening to the concerns of the union members every day since the tsunami.

"Any word on what's going to happen to the factory?"

"I have family here. I can't just pick up and move."

Suzuki tried to encourage them.

"Don't worry. Let's have faith in the company and just keep doing our best."

He was likely trying to encourage himself as much as others. He wanted to believe that NPI wouldn't abandon its employees in Ishinomaki. Now, after so many days of waiting, the company president had told him not to worry. They were going to rebuild the mill. Suzuki finally felt some of his built-up tension melt away.

Haga didn't want to waste any time.

"Let's go take a look," he said, and headed off toward the gates with factory chief Kurata.

When he arrived, he found the factory where he had worked for five years in a state of disarray. Here and there he spotted the roofs of houses that had washed in. Entering the grounds, he saw cars embedded in buildings and logs smashed through closed shutters. Some areas were covered in a sludge of pulp and mud. Devastation was everywhere.

But Haga wasn't focused on the wreckage and debris. He saw that the stock silos were standing straight and that most buildings looked sound. He muttered "okay" several times as he surveyed the area. Kurata watched Haga's reaction, and public relations head Koji Yoshino listened to his CEO's mutterings, reading the emotions behind them.

"All right, let's go check out our beacon of hope," Haga said.

Yoshino knew what he was referring to—the N6 machine.

An enormous log had smashed through the door to the N6 building and still jutted from the entrance. The first floor was covered in mud, and a tangle of fallen electrical lines and chemical pipes blocked the entryway. The men followed a narrow stairway up to the second-floor runway, which looked down on the open space below.

The building was steel-reinforced concrete a twenty-five-meter-high ceiling. Bluish light entered through windows near the ceiling, making the men feel as if they were on the bottom of a pool.

On the floor below them sat the enormous N6 machine. At a length of 270 meters, it was about as long as the battleship Yamato, a fact employees liked to point out with pride. Some ductwork had fallen onto it from the ceiling, but otherwise it looked untouched.

Haga stood in silence, looking down at the machine. The others waited anxiously to hear what he would say.

Finally he nodded and said, "Okay." He smiled. "I think we're good."

Later, Haga stood in front of the clubhouse surrounded by employees with worried expressions on their faces.

"Starting today, NPI will do everything it can to rebuild the Ishinomaki mill," he announced.

After a brief silence, the crowd began to cheer. More than anyone else, the employees born and raised in Ishinomaki had been concerned about the mill's future. They felt the death of NPI—or even of this one factory—could mean the death of the city. Their lives would be ruined. Several people in the crowd began to tear up.

We're going to be okay. Our families are saved, they thought.

"Don't worry about the money," Haga continued. "I've already spoken to the bank."

Those were the words that Kurata most wanted to hear. They were proof that the company was truly dedicated to rebuilding.

Kurata had already begun discussing recovery timelines with other section heads. He had a knack for getting jobs done quickly by looking ahead, and he had been working on the assumption that the company would save the Ishinomaki mill.

"NPI needs this mill," he said later. "I was pretty sure closing it was not an option. They'd invested too much in it for too many years, building it up as their main factory. Cutting it loose would be a short-term solution leading to a long-term death."

There was no turning back once the company decided to make such a huge investment. Haga and Kurata were smiling as they made the announcement, but both knew they were walking on the edge of a precipice. One misstep and they would be responsible for destroying NPI.

They faced a tough situation. Producing paper requires a spotlessly clean environment, but their buildings were filled with mud. Water for industrial use would not be available until summer at best. They couldn't get heavy equipment into any of the buildings, so workers would have to shovel out the mud. Areas with tight pipework would have to be scooped out by hand. Management had no idea how long all of this would take or what kinds of problems they would encounter.

The one thing everyone knew was that recovery in half a year was a major gamble.

Haga had placed his bet on recovery and thrown the dice.

Machine 8 produces approximately 300 tons of paper each day

CHAPTER 4

Machine 8

1

A group of employees' wives took charge of distributing relief goods. After joining them, Murakami's wife Yuriko most often saw her husband when she ran into him by chance while making deliveries. Up until mid-May he was so busy with work that he rarely found the time to come home. He had lost a lot of weight and his face was growing sallow. She thought about telling him to rest up a bit, but decided against it; she knew her husband well enough to know that he wouldn't. His feelings of responsibility toward his work were too strong, and he was too stubborn. All she could do was hope he didn't work himself to death.

Murakami had taken on the task of helping search for corpses on the factory grounds and contacting the police when one was found. One day he made a particularly heartbreaking discovery: the body of a small child. When the child's mother called a few days later, it was Yuriko who answered the phone.

"We just wanted to thank him," the woman said.

When Yuriko told Murakami about the call, he shrugged. "Just doing my job," he said.

"I felt so sorry for him," she told me. "He keeps his feelings bottled up, but I could tell how hard it was for him."

As the weather grew warmer, collecting bodies became extremely difficult. Skin and muscle would slide off of bones when anyone tried to pick them up, so corpses had to be wrapped in blankets and carefully lifted.

In all, forty-one bodies were found on the factory grounds. The last was that of a girl in her early teens, discovered on top of a freight container. Most of the men working that day were fathers themselves. No one spoke, though some sighed tearfully. They took off their helmets and bowed in silent prayer.

We're sorry you had to wait here for so long, all alone. You'll be home soon.

The upper floors of eighteen houses had washed onto the factory grounds, and many came complete with furniture. Murakami and the others would search them for letters or other items bearing the names of their owners. Whenever they found something, they posted notices on bulletin boards at nearby shelters.

One day a family whose house Murakami had discovered approached him at the factory. They had seen one of his notices, they said, and had come to collect their things.

They spent some time gathering what they could from the wreckage. When they were done they stood outside, looking longingly at what once had once been their home and reminiscing about time spent there. After a while they lined up facing the structure. As one the family bowed deeply in thanks, then turned and walked away.

Union leader Suzuki and Nakada from the administration division were visiting homes and evacuation sites to verify the safety of employees who were not on site the day of the earthquake. Because many roads were still impassable, they spent their days on foot.

One day Suzuki heard that a union member's body had been found, so he headed to the gymnasium, which had been turned into a makeshift morgue. When he arrived he met the man's father.

"Help me say goodbye to him, would you?" the father said. He crouched down to the coffin at his feet and opened a small window in it. His son's eyes were still open, staring vacantly into space. They had turned gray, perhaps from being underwater for so long.

Suzuki silently put his hands together and bowed before the body. *I'm so, so sorry,* he thought.

On another occasion, Nakada met with a woman whose son's body had been found, and then later, her husband's. "She said that in a way it was a relief. She'd been worried that her son would be lonely up in heaven all alone, but now he had his father to keep him company,"

Nakada tells me.

Suzuki says he clearly remembers the first cherry blossoms that bloomed after the earthquake. The single men's dormitory stood behind the factory, and the road leading to it was densely lined with cherry trees that bloomed beautifully every year. This year was no exception. When the wind blew, clouds of delicate petals filled the air, like snow against a background of ruins.

"For some reason the blossoms that year were paler than normal," he said. "It almost felt like they had joined us in mourning the dead."

2

By April 1, employees at the Ishinomaki mill were working toward factory chief Kurata's goal of getting a machine running within six months. Finally they had something to work for, a goal to strive for.

Kurata had decided that the N6 machine would be the first one brought back online, so the workers began clearing debris in and around the building housing it. Debris outside the building could be removed using heavy machinery, but everything inside had to be hauled out by hand. They entered the building with trepidation, unsure of what they would find.

Power was still down inside the buildings, so employees used portable spotlights and helmet-mounted lamps to illuminate their work. Large crews first dragged rubbish from the building, then shoveled mud into handcarts and wheelbarrows to haul it out. With water service still down, areas dense with pipes couldn't be washed out; instead, employees cleared them using spoons. It was hard work in a dim, oppressive atmosphere, and the mountains of mud seemed impervious to their efforts.

At times the work crew ran into unexpected problems, such as the huge log that had somehow become lodged near the ceiling—a reminder of the tsunami's fearsome power. No one could figure out how to get it down. In the end they called in a contractor with experience working on tall buildings. He managed to secure a thick rope around the log, allowing them to pull it down.

On April 10, Kurata received a message from corporate headquarters that made him want to scream in anger and frustration:

"We want you to get Machine 8 running first, not N6."

For ten days employees from the Ishinomaki mill and Aimeito, an affiliated company that was helping with the cleanup, had been working to clear the N6 building of mud. The work was backbreaking, and considering the lack of electricity or water it was amazing how clean they'd gotten the place. Kurata couldn't bear the thought of facing his employees with this news.

He continued to exhort them as they went about their tasks, but inside he was consumed with doubt. As a leader, he couldn't show uncertainty or weakness for fear that those under him would lose their confidence. Keeping their spirits up was one of his most important jobs. Still, he could do little more than tell them "good job" as they headed home each day, covered in mud.

He had succeeded in motivating them, but despite his façade of assuredness he mostly felt the solitude of leadership. The fate of the company, the lives of its employees, and even the future of the town he lived in depended on him. Hiding his doubts from those around him was an extra burden.

He wanted the N6 machine running again. It was the symbol of the Ishinomaki plant, and getting it operational would send an unmistakable message that they were back in business. But focusing on N6 was a practical decision as well, because the machine had fewer peripheral devices in need of repair than Machine 8. The N6 machine only used chemical and recycled pulp, but Machine 8 also handled mechanical pulp. That would require much more equipment—and work from his employees—to start producing again.

The sales division at headquarters offered a simple reply to those concerns. "It's paper from Machine 8 that our customers are waiting for. That has to take top priority."

Machine 8 began operating in 1970. It produces fine paper for hard and softcover books, as well as rougher paper for comics. A highly specialized machine, it is capable of manufacturing certain kinds of paper that other mills don't produce. Kurata couldn't deny that the printing industry was waiting for Machine 8. But still…

Kurata was well aware of the ten grueling days the workers had spent clearing the N6 building, but he knew that would carry no weight with the sales division in Tokyo. He also thought about Noguchi, the leader of the N6 team. He was a quiet man and a diligent worker. He likely would not complain were N6 set aside. He had lost his home in the tsunami, but hadn't missed a day of work since. Kurata felt terrible.

I spoke about that time with Kurata's right-hand man, assistant chief Kazumori Fukushima.

"I remember speaking with some kid from the sales department. He said, 'What's the point in making a bunch of paper from the N6 if we can't sell it?' *What a cold bastard*, I thought. Absolutely no consideration for how we felt. It was like a punch to the gut," he told me.

Unable to dissuade headquarters, Kurata called a meeting. He bowed before the other managers in apology.

"Please, forgive me. There's been a change in plans. We have to get Machine 8 running first. I know it's a lot to ask, but we need to change course and direct all of our energy toward getting Machine 8 back up."

Suddenly the list of equipment that had to be repaired was significantly longer. But while many employees felt unhappy about the sudden change in plans, they were still part of the same team. No one rebelled openly. Some did request that the deadline be extended, since ten precious days of the six-month goal had been lost. Yet Kurata held firm.

"Let's see what we can do," he said.

3

In mid-May, the Ishinomaki mill hosted a large meeting focused on reviving NPI. A number of executives from the Tokyo headquarters gathered at the clubhouse to discuss how to proceed with recovery.

The first item on the agenda was a confirmation that Machine 8, not N6, would be the first to be put back into production. Kurata listened grimly, but didn't complain.

Shinichi Sato, director of international sales at the Tokyo headquarters, was one of the executives present at that meeting.

"We knew that switching from the N6 to Machine 8 would hurt morale," he told me. "I was impressed that Kurata went along with it, despite the misgivings I knew he had. I could tell from the expression on his face that he was holding back a lot, especially about how much work the sales division was just brushing aside without regard for the workers' feelings. He wasn't the only one that felt that way. But we really did need Machine 8 running again, no question—it's the paper from that machine that the publishing industry was waiting for. Even today, I believe it was the right decision."

Since the earthquake, Tokyo headquarters had faced the problem of how to keep supplying customers with paper. Although the supply was briefly interrupted, the company was able to quickly resume normal deliveries with the help of other factories and a US subsidiary.

At normal capacity, the Ishinomaki mill can produce around one million tons of paper per year, which equates to a little more than eighty thousand tons per month. Before the earthquake, it supplied around one-fourth of the paper NPI sold domestically.

Eighty thousand tons is a lot of paper. Making up the gap with paper from other NPI plants would have been impossible, yet it had to come from somewhere. Sato reluctantly came to a decision.

"We have to prioritize our customers in Japan. I hate to do it, but I'll tell our customers overseas that we won't be able to sell them paper for a while."

NPI exported paper to a number of countries. Printing companies in Australia were some of its largest overseas customers, but orders also came from New Zealand, India, Taiwan, China, and several countries in Southeast Asia. The thin paper that characterizes *Time* magazine in the United States was produced at the Ishinomaki mill.

Of course, overseas publishers knew about the tsunami. NPI had built up relationships with these clients over many years, and most sent their condolences, along with messages of goodwill saying not to worry about them.

NPI asked both its own factories and other paper companies such as Oji, Hokuetsu, and Marusumi to help make up for the lost production. With their assistance, NPI filled in the gap.

Sato's most pressing concern was filling orders whose scheduled delivery dates were looming. He says the Oji Paper Company in particular was very helpful at that time.

"I visited them when I was out making the rounds of our customers. When I asked if they could help us meet our orders for book-printing paper, they said they would make it a top priority."

Another important machine at the Ishinomaki mill is the N4, which produces paper for fashion magazines, textbooks, and reference books. This led Sato to another difficult decision: repairs to the N6 machine would have to be pushed back even further. Customers couldn't wait any longer for paper from the N4 machine.

Sato has a deep passion for supplying the publishing industry, thanks to his long association with printing companies.

"Paper for printing is the lifeblood of NPI. We're proud of the fact that we've worked with printing companies since before the war, and have a very close relationship with them. So when we thought about the order in which we would bring machines back into production, we had to think of the printing companies first."

When Sato was assigned to NPI's sales division in 1981, his first job was to help develop a new kind of paper for softcover books published by Kadokawa Shoten.

At the time, most paper for softcovers was manufactured by super-calender processing, a method in which the paper surface is treated with chemicals and then placed under high pressures to develop a surface sheen. This also makes the paper very thin, allowing for more pages in a given volume.

But Kadokawa was looking for something new, and wanted to try low-coat-weight paper. In this processing method an ultrathin coating similar to foundation makeup is applied to the paper, giving it a more natural feel. They also developed a method of creating paper in enormous sheets, big enough to produce 128 book pages each. NPI's first attempts met with many problems, but the sales team knew the results would be worth it.

"We worked hard to produce the best books, with the best paper possible," Sato says. "Success would mean providing our customer with something new, something better than what they had before. I think that's the feeling that drives papermakers as we work.

"As you know, a successful paperback can sell tens of thousands, even millions of copies. As a recent example, Kodansha's *The Eternal Zero* started with a print run in the tens of thousands, but now it has sold over four million copies and is still going strong. When you have books like that, it just isn't permissible for the paper supply to dry up. You can't just say 'We'll get it to you, eventually.'

"That's the kind of relationship based on absolute trust that we have with publishers. When we accept a commission to produce the paper for a paperback release, we're making an absolute promise that we'll have the paper for that book, no matter what happens. We've *promised*, right? And without the Ishinomaki mill, we wouldn't be able to uphold that promise.

"So while it was painful to ask them to switch to recovering Machine 8, despite everything they had done, we really had no choice. I think they understood that."

NPI tasked its Fuji mill with manufacturing paper on order for Kadokawa paperback releases at the time of the earthquake, using the company's recipes for that specific paper. But as company executives knew, no two mills can create exactly the same paper.

The biggest reason for this lies in differences in the raw materials used. When the Ishinomaki plant manufactured paper for softcovers, it included mechanical pulp in the blend. The Fuji mill didn't have mechanical pulping equipment, so the paper would have to be produced using only chemical pulp. It might be possible to create a paper of a very similar quality, but the degree of similarity would depend on the skill of the mill's technicians.

Sato was sure that Kadokawa would be nervous about the change in supply, so he prepared for a long series of test runs to make sure the paper was just right. But Kadokawa's chairman stopped him.

"We trust you," he said. "Skip the test runs. Just tell the Fuji plant to start making the paper. We know they'll do a good job."

Those words were proof of the close relationship and trust the two companies had built up over the years. Sato says he was so happy to hear them that he cried.

People in Ishinomaki are doing everything they can to get back on their feet, Sato thought. *We need to do the same.*

Like many other employees in the sales department, he had been at work for days without going home.

4

There was one man who was happy about the new focus on Machine 8: its team leader, Noriaki Sato. He was also the team leader for Machine 7, which was housed in the same building.

When Sato peers keenly out from underneath his work helmet, he is the very picture of a factory floor manager. But he is also a loquacious man with a unique sense of humor who is well loved by both his managers and those he manages. Everyone I talked to agreed that he's perfect for his job.

Sato went to check on his machines as soon as he could after the earthquake. They were housed on the second floor of a steel-reinforced concrete building, above the tsunami's reach. However, they had extensive root systems of pipes, cabling, and electrical conduits that sank down to the lower floor. This vital network supplied the two machines with the power and raw materials they required to operate—and most of it had been ripped out.

"The machines were covered in paper dust, but otherwise they looked fine, like you could just throw a switch and power them up. But the water on the floor below had reached a depth of two meters. I was sure there'd be a body or two down there, but luckily we didn't find anyone anywhere in the building. Still, it was a month before we could make any progress."

As Sato turned to leave the slumbering sister machines on that first day, he thought, *You poor things. We'll get you up and running again, just you wait.*

At first, when N6 was getting all the attention, Sato thought he had plenty of time to get his machines running again. But as time went by, he began to wonder if his time wouldn't come sooner than expected.

He knew the paper that Machine 8 produced was in high demand, especially in the publishing industry. After all, the Ishinomaki mill had previously supplied around 40 % of the paper used in the industry. Other mills could cover for them to some extent, but not fully and not for long.

The more he thought about it, the surer he became that publishers would need his paper and that NPI couldn't leave Machine 8 sitting idle. He began waiting for the day when the baton would be passed. He even began telling those around him, "It's Machine 8 they should fix first, not N6. Just you wait—they'll come around soon enough."

Until March 11 Sato had never considered the possibility of such a large tsunami, not even when the earthquake hit. "I only left the machine building because I was afraid one of the damn things might fall on me," he says.

Sato's cell phone was still working as he evacuated the plant, and he was still in a joking mood when someone from the Iwakuni plant called.

"You still alive?" his colleague said.

"Alive enough to answer the phone, I guess."

"Well are you okay, then? I heard the water was two stories high in Ofunato."

Hearing that, Sato glanced back just in time to see the tsunami hit the city.

His children lived separately from him to attend school and were safely inland. But the home he shared with his parents and an elderly dog was near the sea in the Okawa district, around 24 kilometers north along the Kitakami River. He desperately wanted to get back, but the embankment along the river had given way, cutting off most access.

On the third day after the tsunami the water in some areas was still chest deep, and it had started to snow. Even so, Sato decided he had to get home. If necessary he would borrow a boat from a friend who worked for the fire department.

He filled a knapsack and started off for home. He walked at first and later borrowed a bicycle from someone he knew.

On the way, he saw a young man carrying a baseball bat. As he watched, the youth smashed the window of a convenience store and went in.

"They say the Japanese are generally a law-abiding folk, but I guess there's all kinds of people," he says. "Most people I saw were carrying food, but that kid just had his bat. Not that he was hitting people with it, but still… On the way I passed by some guys from the Self-Defense Force base in Yamagata prefecture, and they gave me some water. It made me happy, seeing that people were coming from all over to help us like that."

The snow started falling more heavily. *I'd better hurry*, Sato thought.

He passed a small store with a handwritten sign: "We have cigarettes." When Sato wandered in, a shopkeeper appeared and eyed him suspiciously.

"Where'd you come from?" he asked.

"I'm local," Sato replied.

"Yeah? What company?"

"NPI."

"No kidding. Used to work there myself. Well you've come quite a ways. Must be cold out there. Let's get something hot into you."

The man began making Sato a cup of coffee.

There's nice folks all around, Sato thought.

When Sato finished his coffee he thanked the shopkeeper and started to leave. The man told him to wait and dashed into the back of the store, where he lived. When he reappeared, he was holding a bundle of spinach.

"Here, take this," he said.

"Why spinach? I have no idea," Sato told me. "I guess he just didn't want to see me leave empty-handed, and that's all he had. It was a kind gesture."

After seven hours of detours around flooded areas, he finally reached the Okawa community center. Inside he met several women he knew. All had stricken expressions.

"What's wrong?" Sato asked. "Did something happen?"

One of the women spoke to him, barely whispering.

"The tsunami... It washed away the kids at Okawa Elementary School."

"What? You've got to be kidding," he said. The woman just looked at him with red eyes.

Sato's children had graduated from there. It was a small school; when his daughter had attended each grade had only two classes. He was still friendly with teachers there, and the parents of students all knew each other. At one time, Sato had served as the chairman of the PTA.

"Oh my god..."

Sato continued toward his home, heavy-hearted.

On the way he saw a group of people huddled together, and joined them to see what was going on. They had found the body of an acquaintance of his, half buried in the freezing mud. Sato recognized the victim immediately, despite his waterlogged and swollen face. Sato was too emotionally paralyzed to feel sad.

"We can't leave the poor guy in the cold like that," he said. "Come on, let's get him out."

The tsunami had destroyed all 108 homes in the neighborhood. Several other neighborhoods had vanished too, with every last home destroyed. The number of dead and missing in this small area alone reached 197.

Sato looked around at what had once been a bucolic landscape where his children had played and ridden bikes. Much of it was now a lake.

When he reached his home, he was relieved to find that it had been just high enough on a hillside to escape the waters. His 22-year old dog happily greeted him. "Hey, Tama. Good to see you safe," Sato said. Then, as if in relief at seeing its beloved owner home safe, the elderly dog lay down and passed away.

Sato soon learned that his wife, who worked at an elderly care facility near the seashore, was safe. Sadly, his aunt, who had lived near them, died in the flood.

5

Sato was excited when he heard that Machine 8 was now first in line to be put back in operation.

"See? What did I say?" he said. "The publishing industry can't live without Machine 8."

Sato grows passionate when speaking about the machine.

"You'd be surprised at the attention to detail that goes into planning for a paperback," he says. "For example, you probably think that they all have white pages, but actually the color varies by publisher. Kodansha's pages have a yellow tinge to them. Kadokawa's are slightly red, and Shinchosha's are very red. Publishers have their own particular colors, which they are very proud of. The color that Kadokawa uses is particularly distinct. We call it 'Kadokawa Orange.'"

He also told me about the steps taken to prevent fading.

"We used to use paper that was slightly acidic," he says. "But the acid in the paper would eventually turn alkaline, causing the paper to discolor. You've seen that in old books before, right? How the pages turn kind of brownish? That's what I'm talking about. So around twenty years ago we switched to acid-free paper, from a pH of around 7 to more like 8. Wood has a neutral pH in its natural state, so it retains its color much better that way. There was a lot of competition at the time to see who could develop the best acid-free paper."

One of Sato's jobs used to be visiting publishers to explain the pros and cons of using acid-free paper. The biggest pro, of course, was its resistance to discoloration. The biggest con was that the precipitated calcium carbonate used in the process caused cut surfaces to stick, so pages wouldn't turn as nicely. It also made the paper cutters in the printing machines dull more quickly.

Thanks to the work of technicians like Sato, however, these demerits ended up being less of a problem than they first seemed. Today, nearly 100 % of the paper manufactured in Japan is acid-free.

Many readers base their image of a publishing house on its paperback books, so publishers are unyielding in their dedication to paperback quality. Consistent paper is part of that. The slightest variations in paper characteristics result in a phenomenon that industry insiders call "tiger striping": when the books are lined up next to each other, the slightly different colors of the paper resemble geological strata. If this happens, papermakers are sure to receive complaints.

The Ishinomaki mill doesn't only make paper for softcover books, however. Sato's daughter Ayana says she remembers her father telling her about this when she was a small child:

"There's all kinds of paper, he said. The paper in my textbooks was made tough, so that it could withstand heavy use, even getting wet. He also told me there was a lot of design behind the paper used in the comics I read. If they used paper like they did in paperbacks the comic books would be too thin, not the kind of thing kids get excited about when they pick them up, so they used thick, soft paper to make comic books thicker. But the paper had to be light too, so that kids could easily take them to friends' houses to share. That's not an easy thing to do, he said."

Ayana told me about her experience as a child.

"When I was a kid, I had no idea what my father did for a living," she says. "Sometimes he'd get calls late at night and rush off to the factory. They must really depend on him, I thought. He always used to grumble about wanting to retire early, but we didn't believe him. I used to joke about it with my brother. He's too addicted to work to ever want to quit, we'd say."

"It's a given that I'll be at the factory when there's a problem, no matter what time it is," Sato says. "It doesn't matter if it's something I can help with directly—my job is to reassure the workers, to let them know I'm the one responsible. But it's the skill of our operators that results in good paper. Skill and hard work."

Machine 7 sits parallel to Machine 8 and is also under Sato's watch. The operators of each were proud of their machines, so they had mixed emotions about seeing one prioritized above the other. The two machines had always worked as a pair, and when problems arose with one the team in charge of the other would pitch in to help make things right again.

Sato asked the Machine 7 team for their support when attention shifted to Machine 8.

"I need you guys to pray that Machine 8 will be back on its feet soon. I need you to fold paper cranes to cheer the team on."

There was some grumbling about what felt like a childish task, but the team cooperated, huddling in groups as they folded cranes. With each one, they said a little prayer—"May Machine 8 recover soon."

Residents in the area began asking Sato about the recovery efforts.

"So when are you guys going to be up and running again?"

"As soon as possible. We're doing everything we can," he would reply.

"Well best of luck, then. The town is depending on you."

Each comment reminded Sato of the town's fondness for and reliance on the mill, reemphasizing the importance of the task at hand.

Sato knows Machine 8 and its quirks well.

"We use this machine for all kinds of paper, twenty varieties at least," he says. "On average we switch output 23, 24 times a month. Lots of the paper varieties also come in different thicknesses, so if you include all those we're talking something like a hundred types."

"You wouldn't think a machine could have a soul," he continues, "but Machine 8 sure seems to have one. Lots of other machines, when they break down they just go down with a crash. But Machine 8 soldiers on, sending us signals that something's wrong. It's almost like a petulant child sometimes, saying, 'You'd better fix me quick, or I'm gonna break!' Then we go in and fix the problem and it's happy again. I think of it as our spoiled princess.

"Once we had a magnitude 5 quake and Machine 7 shut down, just like that. But Machine 8 didn't bat an eye. I was really impressed until later when we had a magnitude 3 quake that didn't seem to bother any of the other machines, but Machine 8 went out like a light. I find that cute somehow.

"Machine 8 is an old one, almost 50 years old now, so the whole thing is analog. The N6 machine is like an autofocus digital camera, where pretty much anyone can just point and shoot to get a decent picture. But Machine 8 is all manual—you've got to twist all the knobs and push all the buttons just right to get what you want. But that's what makes it interesting. When I go into a bookstore, it's easy to find the books with paper from Machine 8. It has its quirks, and just a touch is enough to tell me."

I asked Sato what it's like to find those books.

"It's like being reunited with an old friend," he said. "For a long time after the tsunami we couldn't take baths, couldn't go shopping… Nothing was the way it was supposed to be. So when I loaded the family into the car and we went out, where do you think we went? To bookstores. When everything around me feels like it's falling apart, the place I most want to be is a bookstore.

"We're proud of the fact that we support the printing industry. Whatever they need, we can deliver. No matter what they order, we know we can make it."

6

One day an employee entered a storage area to inspect for damage and gave a shout of surprise. Coworkers who gathered in response were equally startled by what was inside: a massive roll of paper. Undamaged paper in "Kadokawa Orange," packaged and ready for delivery.

How it managed to escape damage from the earthquake and tsunami, nobody knew. Equally mysterious was why it had sat there throughout the extensive cleanup operation without being discovered. But there it sat, like a gleaming gift from the gods.

"We've got to tell sales about this!" someone shouted, and ran off to do so.

Shun Kato at NPI's Tokyo sales division was the first to hear about the discovery. While he knew he should be thrilled at the prospect of having salable product, he was more worried about its condition.

None of the cutters at Ishinomaki were usable, so the entire enormous roll was transported to a cutting facility near Tokyo's Haneda Airport. Kato went there along with Kadokawa's procurement manager to inspect the paper.

"At the time, I couldn't bring myself to be excited," Kato says. "Honestly, on the way to the cutting plant I was filled with a kind of morbid curiosity. I figured the paper just had to be dirty, or creased, or crumpled up somehow. I was afraid to look at it, but at the same time I really wanted to."

When they arrived, they saw a 2-meter diameter, 1.8-meter-tall roll of paper wrapped in orange plastic. Until that moment Kato had only seen the paper he sold in its deliverable form—cut into sheets and bundled in brown laminated paper—so this imposing orange column seemed somehow portentous of ill fate.

But when they pulled back the plastic, Kato and the Kadokawa rep saw only an expanse of smooth, unblemished paper. No matter how closely they examined it, they found no trace of the events that transpired the day it was manufactured. It was perfect, like the silky skin of some goddess. When Kato saw that, he got goose bumps over his entire body.

"Looks good to me," the man from Kadokawa said.

When the paper was cut, they found that the interior of the roll was fine too; the paper was of the same high quality as usual, and there was almost no discard. It was later turned into books, which today sit on shelves of homes throughout Japan.

Raising koinobori carp streamers on a smokestack, April 25, 2011

CHAPTER 5

Passing the Baton

1

Paper machines do not operate in isolation; they rely on various peripheral equipment.

The first devices needing repairs in order to get the Number 8 machine running again were the boilers and turbines. Before that could happen, Tohoku Electric Power Company would have to restore electricity.

Ikeuchi, the manager of the electrical division, didn't think that restoring power to the plant was likely to happen soon.

"Pretty much our entire electrical system had been destroyed," he says. "Almost all of our electrical equipment was on the first floors of buildings, which meant it had all been immersed in saltwater. Easily sixty percent of it was unsalvageable. Only the stuff that was upstairs looked like it might be okay."

Nonetheless, it was up to Ikeuchi to lead the charge toward recovery.

"The first thing we had to do was lay power lines to the boilers. Special high-voltage cables had wound around the exterior of the factory buildings, but they were washed away by the tsunami, mountings and all. Of course new cabling was in demand throughout the disaster area, so getting our hands on any was no small task."

Technical division director Akira Kanamori reported to factory chief Kurata that he was unable to procure the cabling he needed, but Kurata would accept no excuses.

"He really told me off," Kanamori says. "He said, 'Well, where are you looking? Are you even really trying? Have you tried everything? Can you say for sure that there is absolutely no cabling to be had? If you can't find it any other way, find an abandoned factory and rip it out of there!' We were hearing things like that all the time. Section leaders would report that they couldn't do some thing or the other—totally understandable, given the situation—but they would catch hell for it, even when they laid out all the problems they were having. Kurata would make them go through everything they had done and look for other things they hadn't tried yet. They'd always find something, so Kurata would send them off to do that.

"Every day we would give subcontractors impossible schedules. When they came back to us saying they just couldn't get the work done that quickly, Kurata would sell them on his dream of recovery in six months. I guess his passion was infectious, because he was getting them to promise to do jobs in a month that would normally take them half a year. I couldn't believe how quickly they got all the scaffolding up. It should've taken a month, but it felt like it appeared overnight. Our subcontractors really pulled through for us."

The Tokyo headquarters and all of NPI's branches were told that Ishinomaki needed cables. Headquarters broadened the search to overseas and began finding supplies, while Ikeuchi did everything he could back in Ishinomaki.

Electricians began arriving from other NPI factories and affiliated companies throughout the country. Working nearly around the clock, the cobbled-together crew managed to erect utility poles, mountings, and cables along three of the four one-kilometer-long walls that surround the factory.

Another serious problem was how to repair the approximately seven thousand motors that had been immersed in saltwater. Replacing them all was out of the question; in the chaos following the disaster, delivery could easily take years. Instead, Ikeuchi's team hit on a surprising solution.

"We put them in huge vats and boiled them," he says. "That got all the salt out. Then we'd repair the insulation and replace the bearings. Still, you can't do that to seven thousand motors in any reasonable amount of time. So we prioritized them in the order they would be needed and tried to get as many fixed as possible, as fast as we could. We figured that if that wasn't fast enough, then we'd find some other solution. I think that 'let's just see what we can do' attitude was a very productive one."

Kurata was surprised when the first motor sputtered to a start and kept on purring. "I didn't know such a thing was possible," he says. "Of course this was a temporary fix, and eventually we would lose out to rust. But it was good enough for the short term. It let us use whatever would run and replace whatever we had to later on."

To everyone's amazement, the electrical division succeeded in supplying electricity to the Number 6 boiler on July 12, right on schedule—two months before the six-month deadline.

Seeing such a difficult task completed on time excited everyone in the factory and motivated them to work harder at their own jobs. Given the precedent that had been set, no one wanted to be held responsible for delays. This was especially true for teams working on the next suite of equipment that needed repair.

"It was like running a marathon relay," Kanamori says. "Once the baton has been passed it's up to you to get it to the next runner, no matter how tired you are or how hard it is to get there. It was a long, hard run, but dropping out of the race or going too slow meant the whole team would lose, not just you."

"Ordinarily, everybody has their rivals," Kurata says. "But during the recovery everyone was working toward the same goal, which allowed us to come together and move forward in ways that normally wouldn't have been possible."

Now that the first leg of the marathon had been completed, the baton was passed to the engineering division and their chief, Teruhiko Tamai. It was their turn to sprint.

2

With recovery activities fully underway, around one thousand workers were now doing construction work on the factory grounds on any given day. Multiple divisions often had to work in the same space at the same time, increasing the risk of accidents. In addition, they were working in close proximity to heavy equipment, making for an extremely dangerous environment.

Kurata told everyone to be extremely careful and do everything they could to ensure that nobody got hurt. He reviewed safety procedures during morning meetings with managers, who would then go to meetings with their teams and pass on the reminders. Meetings were held again at the end of the day to ensure smooth communication.

"It was such a dangerous environment, and everybody was so tired. It's amazing we didn't have any serious accidents," Kanamori says.

Like the other managers, Tamai held frequent meetings with his team. The engineering division was responsible for fixing the mill's seven boilers, which were housed in the building located closest to the sea. But while large amounts of sand and debris had swept in, the turbines Tamai had been so worried about were sound, with no sign of buckling. Nevertheless, the factory would not run if he couldn't get those turbines spinning again.

Workers in the engineering division were still working seven days a week, although some of the other divisions were now permitted to take days off. The engineering team was responsible for a large number of tasks, including repairing water pipes to and from the factory.

They began work on these tasks before electrical power was restored, so at first they were only able to work during daylight hours. They started with debris removal, an arduous, monotonous chore that left everyone physically and emotionally exhausted. On one of the first days Tamai gathered his team in a circle and spoke to them:

"Listen up. We have a hard job ahead of us, and we're going to get tired. But I want you to promise me one thing—no bad-mouthing your teammates. Some of us are living as refugees. Some of us have lost our homes, even family members. All of us are having a hard time and have things we need to attend to. So when somebody can't show up, I don't want to hear any complaints. Also, some of the other divisions don't have the tight schedule that we do right now. I don't want to hear any griping about that, either. If somebody can't show up, we'll find a way to cover for them. Let's get those turbines spinning again. I want to see smoke coming out of those chimneys."

Everyone in the circle nodded solemnly. Among them were a number of local contractors. They too had been struck by tragedy, but came every day to lend a hand. Since nearly all the local hotels and inns had been destroyed, they weren't able to stay nearby. Tamai was humbled to learn that some had to commute for up to two hours, yet still showed up for work at 5 AM and stayed until dark.

It was a grim time. Ishinomaki had been leveled, as if flattened by bombs. Conversation centered on new confirmations of fatalities— places where more bodies had been found, or the number of deaths in particularly unfortunate families. For some, lending a hand in the factory's recovery was a way of working toward a brighter future. Every bit of debris removed was a tiny yet concrete expression of their hope.

The cleanup seemed to drag on endlessly. Some days were fairly warm, but others were frigid enough that workers lost feeling in their hands and feet.

One day a team member brought a portable barbecue grill to work and used it to make miso soup for everyone. Since most of the normal ingredients were unavailable, it contained only a few small bits of vegetables. Still, it was comforting for the exhausted workers. Tamai was amazed at the difference a cup of thin soup could make.

"We should do this every day," he said. "We should try to make enough for the contractors too. We really need something to cheer everybody up."

The managers all chipped in to create a soup fund to pay for the ingredients. A team member was tasked with shopping, and every day seventy people received a warm bowl of soup.

"We had people out there removing debris from dawn to dusk," Tamai says. "It was hard. Along with ensuring that nobody got hurt, one of our primary tasks was maintaining morale and motivation."

The daily soup became a small pleasure at a time when little enjoyment was to be found. Tamai learned much later that finding the necessary ingredients had been a daily struggle for the team member tasked with shopping, since stores were still under-stocked. He had made their soup every day for almost three months, but never once complained.

Little by little, the mounds of debris shrank. Just when the engineering team thought they were almost done, however, a terrible thing happened.

There are many kinds of boilers, such as those that burn coal and those that burn biomass. Another is a recovery boiler, which burns something called black liquor.

Black liquor is byproduct of pulp production. It contains lignin (the natural "glue" that holds together the fibers in wood) and the chemicals used to dissolve it. This liquid can be reclaimed from the pulping process and concentrated for use as fuel. It is burned in boilers to produce the steam that spins turbines to produce electricity.

In addition to removing debris and mud, the workers had begun removing machine parts for cleaning and maintenance. One day they removed the pump that fed black liquor to the boiler, but failed to notice that the valve had been left open. Concentrated black liquor is a thick, tar-like substance, so nothing spilled out immediately. Thinking there was no problem, the workers left for the day.

When they returned the next morning they found the floor covered in a thick layer of something resembling molasses. Black liquor is alkaline, so touching it irritates the skin. It's also sticky, readily adhering to gloves, clothing, and shoe soles, which increases the risk of tripping.

Because heavy machinery couldn't get inside the building, it would all have to be removed by hand using scoops and ladles.

That was the first of many days spent on hands and knees, scooping up gooey tar. When the workers finally finished, they had filled over five hundred steel drums with the stuff.

On April 25, the boiler's smokestack was still cold. The normal view from the Ishinomaki highway exit, enormous chimneys billowing white clouds of steam, had yet to return.

In the neighborhood surrounding the factory, stray soccer balls and children's shoes were still mixed in with rubble. Patches of ground that had once been yards were starting to grow weeds. When the wind blew through the piles of debris, the air filled with the sound of plastic sheets trapped inside them flapping back and forth. The vinyl tape that marked areas where teams searching for corpses had come and gone snapped in the wind too. Here and there large sinkholes gaped, and those near the ocean filled with gurgling water at every high tide.

The factory's smokestacks—still dormant despite the fact that the employees within were working as hard as they could to get them running again—only added to the gloomy atmosphere.

Kurata turned away from the chimneys to face his second-in-command, Kazumori Fukushima. "Let's raise them today," he said.

Fukushima smiled and said, "Good idea."

They were referring to the enormous *koinobori* carp streamers that Kurata had been raising in celebration of Children's Day since his days at the Asahikawa mill. He and Fukushima had added two handwritten messages to the streamers: "Power of Nippon" and "Now's the time to pull together, Ishinomaki!"

That day, a truck driver called in to the local FM radio station. "I just passed the NPI factory," he said. "They've raised a big *koinobori* on one of their smokestacks. What a great thing to see. It makes me think we're going to pull through."

Fast-forward to 10:30 AM on August 10. The backbreaking work of cleanup and repair had been going on for over three months, with one month left before the six-month recovery deadline.

This was the moment when the fires in Boiler 6 were finally ignited.

A thin line of white steam rose from the top of the smokestack into the clear blue sky. Workers stopped and looked up with excitement. Their factory was coming back. The heart of the mill was starting to beat again. They had raised a signal fire pronouncing that recovery was on its way.

In a meeting with his team the next day, Tamai read out an email he had received from an Ishinomaki resident. The woman who sent it wrote that she had moved away from the town, but she had returned after the earthquake.

"For many years I didn't like the NPI smokestacks," she wrote. "But when I returned home it felt lonely, seeing them with no smoke coming out. Now that it's back I feel encouraged. It makes me feel like we can go on, like we're going to make it."

Tamai's eyes grew moist as he read the letter. When he was done, he saw that many team members were similarly moved.

"But we've still got a lot of work to do," he said. "Let's get to it and have another good day with no injuries."

Everyone nodded firmly.

The engineering department had succeeded in getting the boilers running on schedule, and it was time to pass the baton to the next runner. Tamai had begun to feel a glimmer of hope that the mill would reach its goal of recovery in six months. Everyone had said that short of a miracle it would be impossible, but each passing day was bringing it closer to reality.

3

Several local companies had depended on NPI for their business, and with the Ishinomaki mill dormant some were now teetering on the edge of bankruptcy. The factory no longer needed products delivered or other services provided, so the only way these affiliated companies could keep paying their employees was by hiring them out to assist in debris removal.

For these smaller companies, making sure employees kept their jobs was a top priority. Kenichi Yoshida, an employee at the NPI-affiliated Marutaka Company, was among those threatened with unemployment.

"I figured it was just a matter of time until I lost my job. I never thought they would rebuild the factory. Two weeks after the earthquake there was still no power or water. Our communication lines were shut down, so gossip was our only source of information. Plenty of people said that NPI wouldn't shut down, but who could believe that? They were just repeating things they'd heard from other people," he said.

For several days after the earthquake, Yoshida rode around the area on a bicycle looking at the damage. The rivers he passed over were still clogged with cars. "I'd never seen anything like it," he says.

He visited the Nakazato district, a village situated in a geological depression that filled with water when the tsunami washed in. When he arrived, Japan Self-Defense Force soldiers were using boats to rescue people from the second floors of still-inundated houses.

On March 26, when CEO Haga made his promise of recovery, Yoshida only half believed it. He had seen too many dead bodies to have much hope.

"There were people coming back down from the hills, walking past bodies and crying 'I'm so sorry, I'm so sorry' as they did. Nobody wanted to talk about it so it didn't make the papers, but the hell they experienced was there all the same."

His company tasked him with the job of recovering rolls of paper that had been washed out from the mill. These large spools of paper were around one meter in diameter and eighty centimeters tall, resembling giant rolls of toilet paper. If fully unrolled, the paper in a single roll would span fifteen kilometers, and even when dry they weighed around eight hundred kilograms each. Yoshida's job was to collect rolls that had been soaked in mud and seawater, making them far heavier than usual—between two and three tons, he guessed.

The job began with a phone call; someone had called to report that a roll of paper had washed into his yard and request that NPI remove it. Since NPI was the only paper company in town, there was no question as to whether it was theirs. The company immediately dispatched a few employees to haul the paper away.

What at first seemed to be one minor job soon ballooned into a much bigger undertaking, however. As word spread that NPI would come to collect paper rolls, hundreds of residents began to request the service.

The task often involved more than simply driving to the site and loading the paper onto a truck. Many of the rolls were entangled in nests of debris, and at first workers did their best to haul off the debris along with the paper. But these gestures of goodwill added significantly to their workload. Soon, a rumor spread that NPI would remove debris if you asked them to.

NPI began receiving requests from nearby factories, and before long workers found themselves assisting in the cleanup efforts of other companies. At times, NPI even became the target of pent-up anger and frustration. Some residents blamed the company for the destruction of their homes, claiming that if the paper rolls hadn't washed out of the factory, their homes would have been fine. Those responsible for answering these angry phone calls could do nothing but apologize.

Some of the rolls had come to rest standing up like tree stumps, while others lay on their sides. The latter could be removed relatively easily, but the former were much more difficult to deal with.

"As you can imagine, paper that's been soaked in seawater becomes very soft," Yoshida says. "But it's also very heavy, so the bottom would split and spread out and adhere to the ground. That made it impossible to tip rolls over onto their side. When they'd landed inside people's homes it was impossible to bring in heavy machinery, so we just had to rip them apart by hand, little by little."

The areas that Yoshida and his team visited had been directly hit by the tsunami. For the most part, they were now ghost towns crisscrossed with toppled traffic signals and utility poles. The sky above them seemed somehow larger than normal, Yoshida thought.

As the crew drove down a path carved between piles of debris, the only movement aside from theirs was that of the four- and five-man teams of NPI and Marutaka employees. Nobody else was in sight. The only sounds were the truck's engine, the slamming of its doors as they got out, and the crunch of broken things underfoot as they walked. The silence around them seemed to amplify these sounds and the occasional sea breeze rustling through the wreckage.

They entered a home where an automobile had plunged through a wall into the living room, forming the major component of a pile of debris that included a roll of NPI paper. It had been soaked in water and swelled to far beyond its normal size. It was covered in a mix of mud and sodden livestock feed that had washed in from another factory.

Yoshida started up the weed cutter he had brought and began slicing into the layers of wet paper. When he had gouged out a deep slit, he stuck his fingers in and pulled back a chunk of paper. As he did so the air filled with a powerful stench of rot and a dense black swarm of flies, which rose up like a cloud in a sandstorm. Yoshida frantically waved his hands in front of his face, trying to clear them. The buzzing cloud of flies was so thick he could feel them through his gloves as he swept his hands back and forth.

The workers briefly retreated, overwhelmed with nausea from the smell. When their gagging died down, they lined up to form a relay between the roll and the truck. The man in front would rip out a chunk of paper and pass it to the end of the line, where it was bagged and thrown onto the back of the truck. The hard labor left their hands, shoulders, and backs aching.

When they were finally done, they piled into the truck and drove down the empty road toward the next reported location of a paper roll. As they were driving, Yoshida spotted a small group of men carrying golf clubs and baseball bats. As he watched they began attacking a vending machine that had once sold drinks. When it finally cracked open they gathered around it, fishing within for drinks and small change. Yoshida clenched his jaw as he watched this petty act. Just the other day he had queued up at 4:30 AM, waiting with everyone else in line to get some juice for his grandchild. He wished there was some way to report the thieves, but they and his team were the only people around for miles. He turned away from the window.

On another day they were assigned an even more difficult recovery task. A roll of paper had been found in one corner of a nearby factory, tangled with at least twenty cars and trucks. To recover that one roll of paper, the company had procured a bulldozer, a four-ton truck, a truck-mounted crane, and a garbage truck.

One of Yoshida's subordinates had lost his wife, another his cousin. Several had lost their homes. In an effort to spread a little cheer and make the work less of a burden, he began egging them on in a thickly exaggerated version of the local dialect.

"It's another beautiful day! Let's get to it, the company is counting on us!" "Hop to, hop to!" "Watch it there, son, don't hurt yourself!"

His antics had the intended effect, and the workers began smiling and laughing. However, his attempt at levity was not appreciated by everyone. A woman approached them from a nearby house and yelled, "Just what do you think is so funny about all this?"

They stopped what they were doing and turned to face the angry woman. All humor instantly evaporated. Yoshida bowed to her.

"I'm very sorry," he said.

After she stalked off he turned to the other workers. "We all deal with grief in our own way, I suppose. Poor thing."

The crew silently finished the job. When they were done they had hauled away not only the paper roll, but the rest of the debris as well.

Now and then, the team would find paper in perplexing locations. Once, they found a roll perched atop a thin cinderblock wall. They found another sitting alone in an interior room of a house. One had wedged itself into a factory drainage pipe like a cork in a bottle. The most distant roll they found was sitting near the highway exit leading to Ishinomaki port, about five kilometers away.

One day Yoshida entered a house to collect a roll of paper. When entering homes he normally avoided looking at personal possessions, but on that day he happened to notice a family portrait sitting on a table. He was surprised to see that it was a photograph of a friend's parents. As he looked at the photo of the smiling couple, he remembered having heard that his friend had lost both of his parents in the tsunami. Now he was standing in what had once been their home.

Wiping away a tear, he pressed his hands together before him and bowed toward the photograph.

On another day Yoshida was using heavy equipment to clear away a mountain of debris and bundled recycled paper when he glimpsed what looked like hair. He hoped it was a doll, but it turned out to be a human corpse.

"This was three or four months after the earthquake, and we were still finding bodies. I'm just glad we were finally able to bring some closure to their loved ones. Even now there are around twenty-five hundred people that haven't been found. I can only hope that they somehow make it back to their families."

Another difficult task was cleaning up pulp, which now resembled tissue paper inadvertently thrown in with the laundry. A river of pulp had broken through the storm doors of a nearby house along with several automobiles, leaving a 50-centimeter-thick layer of muck. Digging into the pulp uncovered a whitish substance that gave off a powerful sweet-sour odor of decay.

Attempting to scoop up the wet, rotting pulp with shovels did little more than scrape a thin layer off the top. Instead, workers had to drive the edges of their shovels into it over and over until a crack appeared. Doing so invariably released a swarm of flies. Yoshida and his team battled on, chipping away chunks of rotten pulp to load into wheelbarrows and haul outside.

Even during the hardest days, however, there were some bright spots. Yoshida says he will never forget the cold day that staff from Okaido Elementary School brought the team hot lunches, or the warmer afternoon when the owner of the house where he was working gave him some ice cream to thank him for his hard work. They were small gestures, but ones that he was very thankful for.

What cheered him on the most, however, were the kind comments that people would offer in passing.

"So NPI's going to rebuild, eh? Glad to hear it. I don't know what we would do without you guys."

These simple words were enough to make him tear up.

"Even I wasn't really sure we could do it," he said. "I kept thinking about how we would get by without the mill. But every day, little by little, the factory grounds were getting cleaned up. Every day we got a little deeper in, and things got a little closer to normal. I started to imagine getting our old lives back. Everyone was so happy to see the progress."

I asked Yoshida what event during that time made him the happiest.

"Well remember, for a long time we didn't have water or power," he replied. "It wasn't just dark in the town, it was pitch black. You couldn't see a thing. People were telling all these stories about how bad things had gotten, and the nights were just scary, so scary.

"Then one evening everybody started buzzing with excitement about something. I asked what was going on, and they said the power was coming back on. I rushed out onto the street, and I could see it happening. Far off in the distance, the lights were coming on one area at a time, *pop pop pop*. It was flat around there, and dark, so we could see it from really far off. *Pop pop pop*, more areas lighting up, still off in the distance but coming closer and closer.

"I can't tell you how happy that made me."

The cleanup continued. Eventually, Yoshida's team grew to include fifty workers. Later, volunteers from across the country joined them as well.

"I don't have the words to express my gratitude to the volunteers. They did such a great job."

In all, NPI helped clean up 243 sites outside of its mill. The job had seemed like it would never end, but with the help of a small army of volunteers, it finally did.

The NPI Ishinomaki baseball team after qualifying for the 2013 Intercity Baseball Tournament finals

CHAPTER 6

The Baseball Team

1

Among the muddy employees clearing debris in the months after the disaster were six new members of the company baseball team. One was Takashi Goto, who five years earlier had earned a reputation as one of Japan's top high school baseball players. (In Japan, high school baseball is a beloved spectator sport whose annual tournaments rival professional games in popularity).

The final game of the 2006 Japanese High School Baseball Championship was a particularly thrilling match, and fans nationwide were glued to their television sets and radios. Goto was the captain of the Waseda Jitsugyo High School team, which was facing off against Komazawa Tomakomai High School. Pitching for Komazawa was Masahiro Tanaka, who now plays for the New York Yankees.

The game lasted a grueling 3 hours 37 minutes, and after fifteen innings the two teams were still tied. This triggered a rematch—the first invocation of this rule in 37 years. In the seventh inning of the rematch, a timely hit by Goto gave Waseda a 4-to-1 lead, but Komazawa managed to score two points in the ninth inning, putting Goto's team just one ahead.

With two outs and one run to tie, it was Tanaka's turn in the batter's box. He put up a good fight, but Goto struck him out, giving Waseda the victory. All of Japan roared at the spectacular display of sportsmanship.

Tanaka joined the professional-league Rakuten Eagles right out of high school. The pitcher on Goto's team entered Waseda University, then joined the Nippon Ham Fighters, another professional team. Goto too attended prestigious Waseda University and joined NPI's Ishinomaki amateur baseball team after graduating. (Many large companies in Japan have amateur teams, sometimes hiring employees with the sole intent of putting them on the team.)

Now Goto found himself surrounded by rubble.

On March 11, 2011, just weeks after graduating from college and joining NPI's Ishinomaki team, Goto was participating in the Sports Nippon baseball tournament. The team had experienced a disappointing loss in the semifinals, and players were spending the afternoon back at their hotel in a Tokyo suburb. When the powerful shocks of the earthquake hit, they turned on their televisions to see what had happened. They quickly learned that the epicenter was in the Tohoku region.

Team members with family in Ishinomaki loaded some relief goods onto the team bus and set off immediately for home. The others, including Goto, were told to wait in Tokyo until further notice.

"Since our cell phones weren't working, the only way to get news of what was happening was from the TV," Goto says. "We definitely couldn't play baseball, so other than eating and sleeping, we just watched the news. Our lives were kind of taken over by the earthquake, even though we weren't actually there."

Eventually the players were transferred to the dormitories at NPI's Fuji plant, about 100 kilometers from Tokyo. They ended up staying there for two weeks.

It was a period of unease for all of Japan. Out of respect for the victims of the terrible tragedy in Tohoku, many people stopped listening to music or participating in other forms of entertainment. Goto's teammates began to whisper amongst themselves: "Now's not really the time for baseball. I wonder if NPI will keep the team active."

Goto began receiving emails from former classmates asking how he was doing. He had no idea how to respond, because he had no idea what would happen to him.

With nothing else to do, Goto and his teammates began practicing baseball on a nearby beach. They were still officially a company baseball team—for now at least—so baseball was part of their job. Even so, they found it difficult to get motivated.

* * *

The NPI Ishinomaki baseball team got its start in 1986, when the mill still belonged to the Jujo Paper Company. At first its players were selected from local high school students and employees who had played some baseball in school. However, the top teams in the amateur leagues actively scouted skilled college athletes and high school students who had made their mark at the national championships. This made it difficult for the NPI team to compete at a national level, and their win–loss record reflected that.

As NPI's executives knew, there were many good reasons for a company to have a baseball team. The team helped create a feeling of solidarity among employees and contributed positively to the entire community. Competing in the Intercity tournament brought nationwide name recognition to Ishinomaki, and local sports education got a boost when team members took part in events for kids.

Nonetheless, the late 1990s and early 2000s was an era of budget cuts and corporate slimming. Even before the 2011 earthquake executives often questioned the value of the baseball team, and its continued existence was by no means assured—especially if it didn't start winning some games.

In 2009 the factory head who preceded Kurata decided it was time to get serious about the baseball team. To that end he summoned Yasuo Kimura, a former captain for the NPI Ishinomaki team.

"The factory chief told me to see what I could do, but that if we didn't see results they'd have to shut the team down. It was sink or swim," Kimura told me when I met him. His thin face and glasses gave him an intellectual, sober air.

Kimura put on a baseball uniform for the first time in sixteen years and headed out to see what he had to work with.

What he found surprised him. Team members were working on the factory's three-shift schedule and showing up for practice after a hard day of work.

"Players on the night shift would work from 10:00 pm until 7:00 am, have a meal and a quick nap, then show up for practice at 9:00 am. I don't see how anyone could compete in serious baseball under physical and mental pressure like that. Of course they were playing like rank amateurs! I worked things out with management to allow them to work a factory shift in the morning and show up for practice in the afternoon."

Another problem was that participation in the team was something of a casual affair. "Players who got tired of being on the team would just resign. That's not an attitude that someone who's serious about baseball can have. The players that we scouted knew they were being hired to play baseball, that that was their job, so they would never just up and quit. After all, these are guys who hoped to make it into the major leagues someday. We went from having players resign from the team to cutting players from the team because we needed to make room for more skilled athletes."

In addition to changing the team members, Kimura also changed the stage on which they competed. He wanted to bring his team face-to-face with better athletes to show them the level that they were striving for.

Amateur teams compete to participate in two main tournaments, the Intercity Baseball Tournament and the somewhat less prestigious All-Japan Tournament. Kimura set winning one of those as his goal.

When I asked him if doing so helped build team spirit, he shook his head.

"No, no it didn't," he said. "I don't think they believed anything like that was possible."

A long series of regional events leads up to the major tournaments. The first that Kimura's team participated in was called the Babe Ruth Cup, and their first opponent in that series was Seino Transportation, a powerhouse team that often made it to the finals in the Intercity tournament.

The result was a crushing loss. NPI was unable to score a single point, and the game was ended in the seventh inning by invoking the mercy rule. Spectators likened the experience to watching pros play against Little Leaguers.

"I remember we once played a practice match against Rakuten's farm team at the Ishinomaki Civic Field," Kimura says, shaking his head and smiling bitterly. "NPI's baseball team wasn't popular enough to draw a crowd, but the Rakuten pro team has many fans, so the bleachers were packed. Rakuten scored around ten runs in just the first inning. We were thinking, 'Please, make it stop. Make it stop!' but the hits just kept coming. I'd go out to the pitcher's mound to change pitchers, and a chorus of booing and heckling would rise up. It was just awful."

Still, NPI didn't lose all of its matches. By around July of that year they began gaining traction. They made it as far as the elimination rounds for the Intercity tournament and missed getting in by a hair. Making it that far was enough to change the team's attitude. The players started to believe they had a shot at making it big.

When Kimura became head coach in 2009, the team had only nineteen players. During his second season he began traveling with his assistant coach to scout for new talent and eventually signed seven new players, including some from the Nissan team. One team member dropped out, bringing the total to twenty-five players. When Kimura looked at his team, now more experienced and benefitting from new talent, he was sure they could take their game to a higher level.

2010 was the team's 25th anniversary and the mill's 70th. NPI played exhibition games against strong regional teams like Japan Railways East Tohoku and 77 Bank, and when they did so it was hard to ignore the scornful looks coming from their opponent's dugout. Yet Kimura knew his team had changed. If opponents were expecting the NPI of the past, they were in for a surprise.

NPI was matched with 77 Bank in the qualifying round for the 2010

Intercity tournament. 77 Bank was ranked much higher than NPI, but a walk-off home run by NPI's Takuya Koike in the tenth inning gave NPI a dramatic underdog victory.

"I'd been playing baseball for many years, but I'd never seen a game like that. It was a perfect win, and it showed everyone that we were ready for the national stage," Kimura says.

The national tournament was scheduled to take place in Tokyo Dome. Since this would be NPI's first appearance in a national tournament, headquarters pulled out all the stops to support the team. 13,000 employees and family members from NPI and client companies came to Tokyo for the game, traveling either on the twenty-some buses NPI had chartered or by bullet train. The NPI Ishinomaki team was representing not only their company and their city, but the entire Tohoku region.

Unfortunately, they lost in the first round—but they'd nevertheless managed to imprint the name of NPI and Ishinomaki on the national consciousness.

The team continued to improve during the remainder of that year. Kimura signed his first professional player, and in employee break rooms and pubs all around Ishinomaki people were talking about the baseball team. "2011 will be a very good year," they'd say. "There's no stopping us now."

The first official games of the 2011 season were held in March as part of the Sports Nippon Cup tournament. This was the series the NPI Ishinomaki team was playing in on March 11, the day the earthquake struck.

2

Back in Ishinomaki, people began wondering aloud if the baseball team would be disbanded. It was still unclear whether the plant itself would be rebuilt, so no one would have been surprised if NPI decided to pull out of baseball. Most people in town, however, wanted the team to remain intact.

In the weeks and months following the disaster, entertainment was limited, and survivors relied on four things to keep their spirits up: cigarettes, alcohol, books, and baseball. Still, times were tough. If NPI decided to rebuild the Ishinomaki mill, the company would need tens of billions of yen. Townspeople felt sorry for the players—especially since they had finally become *good*—but the general consensus was that playing baseball when so many people had lost their homes and families was somehow inappropriate. They steeled themselves for the inevitable announcement that the team would be shut down.

The decision would be made by factory chief Kurata. Oddly enough, Kurata had faced a similar decision earlier in his career—he dreaded a repeat of that experience.

There had once been a baseball team at the NPI Asahikawa mill in Hokkaido, where Kurata worked before coming to Ishinomaki. The Asahikawa team was established in 1978, when the mill still belonged to Sanyo Kokusaku Pulp, and for a time it was quite popular. Locals even had a pet name for the players: "The Studs of Northern Hokkaido." In 1992 the team made it to the all-Japan tournament, but they never managed to break into the Intercity finals.

The Asahikawa factory was hit hard by the economic downturn of the early 1990s. For a time, the company was unable to hire new employees, which meant that aging players could not be replaced with fresh, young talent. The team's prospects grew increasingly bleak.

As part of a corporate restructuring in 2000 the Asahikawa team was merged with the Ishinomaki team and some of its members were transferred there. The staff member with administrative control over the team at the time was none other than Hiromi Kurata.

The decision to disband a baseball team with a long history is not an easy one. The Asahikawa team played its final match against NTT Hokkaido in the preliminary round of the Hokkaido regionals. Kurata was in the dugout that day, and he described the scene in a 2013 memoir, *538 Days of Triumph and Despair*:

"From some point around the fifth inning, everyone was playing with tears in their eyes. I doubt they could see the balls that were being pitched to them. It was like that for the rest of the game. When it became clear that the baseball team didn't have a future, we decided to let everyone go as soon as possible, so that at least the younger players would still have an opportunity to go play somewhere else, but it sure made for a rough final game."

When the game was over, Kurata headed out to the pitching mound to bid farewell to the team and its fans. Afterward the players lined up along the first base baseline, took off their hats, and bowed deeply to him. It was a scene he would always remember.

Now, ten years later, he found himself in a similar predicament. Once again the future of a baseball team was being called into question on his watch.

When he took over at Ishinomaki in 2010, he had been relieved to find one player on the team who he recognized: Naotoshi Goto. Goto had joined the Asahikawa plant and its baseball team straight out of high school, the very year the team was shut down. In the hopes of preserving some kind of future for the youth, Kurata had transferred him to the Ishinomaki team. Now he was nearly thirty. Seeing him playing on the Ishinomaki field called up many emotions for Kurata, but mostly relief that Goto had been able to keep playing. He was a valued player, too—it was he who scored the tying home run in the 2010 match that put Ishinomaki in the Intercity finals.

Goto's love and dedication to baseball were evident. He was part of the reason Kurata became an avid fan of the team after coming to Ishinomaki.

In 2011, the NPI Ishinomaki team lost one of its best players to the Yakult Swallows, but the season nevertheless looked promising. On March 8 they beat the mighty Toyota team 7–8 in a Sports Nippon tournament match. On the following day they dragged Nippon Express into overtime, scoring an amazing five points in the eleventh inning to seize victory. Their next game was against Japan Railways East, widely acknowledged to be the stronger team, but NPI rookie pitcher Kida shut them down for the win.

This series of upset victories left no room for doubt: the NPI baseball team was now a force to be reckoned with. They had demonstrated their prowess to the entire country and were getting the recognition they deserved.

The semifinal match was scheduled for 10:00 AM on March 11.

The company rushed to charter buses to take supporters from Ishinomaki to Jingu Field in Tokyo. They urged Kurata to come with them, but Kurata demurred at first. As the day approached, however, Kurata began to have second thoughts—it really would be great to go cheer on the team. Flipping through a bullet train schedule he saw that a new super express line had begun operating just the week before, and that's how he ended up in Tokyo that fateful day.

The weather was clear and sunny, and the NPI team put up a good fight. In the end, however, they lost their semifinal match to NTT West, 5–3. Kurata was satisfied all the same; the team had played well.

After the match he paid his respects to the lead coach and NPI staff who had come from headquarters, then boarded the bullet train, alone, to return. He was scheduled to arrive at Sendai Station at 2:37 PM, which would give him enough time to get back to the factory and finish his work for the day.

A company-owned Lexus was waiting for him at Sendai station. He climbed in and told the driver to take him straight to the factory. He felt the first tremors at 2:46 PM, just as they were leaving the vicinity of the station.

Kurata didn't want to disband the baseball team.

This was partly because he didn't want to experience the pain he'd gone through with the Asahikawa team, but there were other reasons as well. For one, the team members were some of his best employees: polite, hardworking, and excellent team players. They set an example for the rest of the company to follow.

No doubt some of his colleagues considered a sports team an unnecessary waste of resources at a time when the factory, and even the entire company, was in such dire straits. Kurata knew that a good argument could be made along those lines. Nonetheless, he worried about the message he would send by casting aside the company's beloved team merely because business wasn't doing so well and resources were needed for the recovery.

If one part of Kurata's job was saving the mill, another part was saving the baseball team. He was convinced that giving up on the team would be the same as giving up on the entire factory, and he refused to do either.

When CEO Haga came to Ishinomaki on March 26 to announce that NPI would rebuild the mill, members of the media and the general public asked him again and again what would happen to the baseball team. This surprised Haga. People were hungry and exhausted, toiling every day to clear wreckage and debris. They had lost homes, friends, and family—yet the fate of the baseball team appeared to be one of their most pressing concerns. Clearly the residents of Ishinomaki loved their team.

So Haga nodded solemnly and said, "Of course we'll keep the baseball team."

Overjoyed employees immediately sent emails and made phone calls to give the good news to head coach Kimura and the team members, who were still unable to return to Ishinomaki.

Just three years earlier, those players had been the pitiful subjects of ridicule, getting booed off the field in called games. But they hadn't given up. They had grown stronger and stronger, defeating increasingly powerful opponents, and now they were a source of pride. They were living proof of the silver lining around every dark cloud—something that the residents of Ishinomaki in 2011 sorely needed.

On March 30, the team members staying at the Fuji mill dormitories—including Takashi Goto—were finally able to return home. Goto had spent only one week in Ishinomaki before the disaster, in early February. After that, he had been shipped off to baseball camp.

When he first saw what had become of the town, he was at a loss for words. Nothing was the way he remembered it. The scale of devastation far exceeded anything he had imagined.

The company had not yet announced when baseball practice would resume, and it was too uncomfortable a question for Goto to ask. For the time being, all he could do was work alongside the other muddy employees, clearing debris.

The entire country was in a mood of restraint, so something as frivolous as practicing baseball would surely be met with unkind stares. This just wasn't the time or place. Still, Goto had spent many years building up his abilities, so the urge to maintain a practice schedule was nearly overwhelming.

Goto surprised Noriaki Sato and the others when he showed up for work one day and introduced himself. "I said, *That* Goto? Our new star player?" recalls Sato. "The poor kid was so new to the company that nobody even recognized him, and look at the mess he was thrown into. But he was strong and a good worker. A great guy."

One of the major hardships for Goto was the food. "All we had to eat were frozen dinners, canned mackerel, stuff like that for every meal," he says. As an athlete who had just graduated from college, this sudden departure from his previous meal regimen was particularly harsh.

He also found it difficult to sleep at night. "The window in my dorm room faced south, and it was pitch black out there at night," he says. Outside his window was a cliff, and at the bottom of that an area that had burned to the ground. Not a soul could be seen, and without electricity the nights were pitch black. "When I opened my window at night, I could swear I heard faint voices coming from the darkness, like moaning or crying." Goto is not the only one who experienced this; others too reported hearing voices and complained of being unable to eat or sleep well.

But most painful of all was not being able to play baseball. "I still didn't feel comfortable asking for practice time, but after all we'd been hired to play baseball. I felt like baseball was my contribution to society, so I didn't want to give it up. If the powers that be decided they weren't going to keep the team that would be one thing, but as long as we were around practicing was part of my job. Still, recovering from the disaster was clearly important too, so I figured practice could wait until we'd cleaned the place up a bit."

One day someone from the Ishinomaki Chamber of Commerce contacted head coach Kimura to tell him that a group of well-known entertainers was organizing a soup kitchen. Could the NPI team come lend a hand? Seeing this as an excellent opportunity to give back to the town, Kimura gladly offered his team's assistance. For ten days they helped out with everything from guiding traffic to washing dishes.

"Clearing debris is depressing work," Goto says. "You spend the whole day looking down, and at times it seems like the job will never be done. But working in the soup kitchen was great. We met lots of people who cheered us on and told us they were rooting for us. Seeing how happy we were making people made me really glad I played baseball."

Coach Kimura developed a plan to collect donations of baseball equipment from across the country to give to children who had lost their homes. "There were a lot of kids who wanted to play sports but couldn't because their equipment had all washed away," Goto says. "We wondered if we couldn't help them replace what they'd lost and cheer them up by playing ball with them, so we held a baseball workshop and handed out the donated equipment to everyone who came. The kids' faces reminded me of how excited I was when I got my first glove. It was a wonderful feeling to share that joy."

In May, factory chief Kurata figured it was about time for the team to start practicing again.

The players had been working hard to help with recovery efforts, and things were slowly getting under control. Even so, practicing in Ishinomaki was out of the question. With residents still under so much stress, the team could face negative repercussions if they appeared to be treating the situation lightly. Resuming practice would have to be handled carefully.

On a business trip to Tokyo, Kurata accompanied chairman of the board Masatomo Nakamura and CEO Haga to a grilled eel restaurant. He broached the topic as they waited for their food, watching their reaction closely.

"So I've been wondering, when should we start back up with baseball practice?" he said.

"As soon as possible, of course. Now, if you have a place," replied Haga.

Chairman Nakamura nodded. "The Asahikawa plant has a nice field. How about you take them there?"

"Relocate the whole team to Hokkaido? That won't be cheap," Kurata said.

"Let us worry about that."

Kurata felt a heavy weight lift from his shoulders. The chairman and the CEO had confirmed that they were as dedicated to protecting the team as he was. Now he just had to make sure they didn't regret their support.

In May 2011, the NPI Ishinomaki baseball team was relocated to Asahikawa. Back at the factory everyone was hard at work clearing mud, but Kurata was prepared to ignore any grumbling that might arise.

News that the team was resuming practice soon reached the media, which reported this as a sign of recovery in the Tohoku region. This put additional pressure on the players to do well.

One player felt unable to leave his family behind and relocate to Hokkaido: Naotoshi Goto, the transplant from the Asahikawa mill team who by now had been playing for Ishinomaki for ten years. On the day of the earthquake his wife had taken their newborn baby to a hospital, after which they had lost contact. For a period of several days Goto was unable to make it back to Ishinomaki to ensure that his family was safe. He knew all too well the pain that a long-term separation would bring.

"I could understand how he felt," says Kimura. "Thankfully everyone was safe and sound, but we were still experiencing strong aftershocks. It's totally understandable that he wouldn't be comfortable leaving his wife and baby just so he could go practice baseball. I didn't want him to leave the team, though, so I told him to stay in shape and work out whenever he could, and that he could rejoin us when we came back."

However, Goto decided to resign from the team later that year, citing the frequent road trips that kept him away from his family.

After the team had gotten in some practice at Asahikawa, Kurata told them to tour the other NPI factories throughout Japan to thank them for their support. The team visited factories in Fuji, Yatsushiro, and Iwakuni, holding practice matches with other local teams.

"At first it was a gloomy time for us, but that changed as we progressed through our tour of the country," says Takashi Goto. "When we visited factories the employees would greet us with cheers and banners urging us on, which really lifted our spirits. We'd been haunted by the question of whether we should be playing baseball at a time like that, but after a while we got to where we couldn't wait for our next real match. We wanted to serve as a symbol of recovery. It really helped to pull us together as a team."

One day in August, someone at the Ishinomaki mill found amongst the rubble a tattered flag depicting a blue winged lion—the Blue Lion victory banner presented to the NPI Ishinomaki baseball team when they won the Tohoku regional championship in the Intercity tournament. It had been submerged in the tsunami and covered in mud, fading from its previous deep blue and losing most of its golden fringe. NPI returned the flag to the Japan Amateur Baseball Association, which has since put it on display at Kyocera Dome as a symbol of the recovery of the Tohoku region.

3

The 2011 season was a difficult one for the baseball team, resulting in a win–loss record that did not reflect their previous performance. But by September things were starting to look up, to the extent that little by little the team was able to resume its previous practice regimen in Ishinomaki. The team members looked to 2012 as their comeback season, the time when they would reclaim the Blue Lion banner and once again compete in the Intercity tournament. Under coach Kimura's leadership, they set off to do just that.

They started with a string of handy victories in the preliminaries, but lost their first 2012 game in the regional finals by just one run and experienced another close loss in their second game.

"It was a tough year," Kimura says. "The players were in fine shape and did well. We missed taking the regional title by just one point. Only I can take the blame for our loss—something our fans didn't let me forget."

They were now out of the running for the Intercity tournament, leaving the all-Japan tournament as their last chance for a league victory that year.

"But again, it was a narrow loss for us," Kimura says. "I really feel like I let the players down."

Goto says that he felt something had changed among his teammates. "Everyone seemed clumsy and awkward for some reason. It was really hard to watch them from the bench."

A factory employee who watched from the stands agrees: "All the fans noticed it. The players were stiff, definitely off their game. We were whispering to each other, wondering what the problem was."

"At the time everyone just said we weren't quite there yet and left it at that, but now that I look back on it, I think a lot of it was the pressure," Goto says. "We'd started thinking of ourselves as part of this 'symbol of recovery,' which was a heavy load to bear. It threw us off. Nobody talked about it outright, but it was definitely there, this invisible pressure.

"Team morale was high and I think we were ready for it physically, but at an individual level we were all carrying emotional burdens that prevented us from getting into the zone. We didn't have that level of psychological freedom that lets you really excel."

Goto says that returning to work after their defeat was hard.

"Coworkers who I was on good terms with just teased and joked about it, but others definitely seemed to be holding me at a distance because I was on the team. That's the price of failure, I suppose."

Ishinomaki viewed from the top of Mt. Hiyori

CHAPTER 7

The Barkeep's Tale

1

When I write nonfiction books, I often feel as if I am not so much actively writing as becoming a conduit for the force of the story I am relating. That was certainly the case with this project.

It started in 2012, exactly one year after the earthquake, when Hayakawa Publishing vice president Atsushi Hayakawa visited the NPI Ishinomaki mill for a tour. He was so overwhelmed by what he saw when factory employees guided him through Ishinomaki and neighboring Onagawa that he found himself at a loss for words. "Neither 'thank you' nor 'good luck' seemed quite appropriate," he said.

Although he felt that human language was an inadequate tool for conveying the devastation inflicted by a natural disaster of this magnitude, he also felt that creating a record of what had happened at the factory was very important.

In the spring of 2013, an editor at Hayakawa contacted me to ask if I would write a book about the NPI Ishinomaki mill. The hope was that I would be able to somehow find the words to describe what Hayakawa had felt when he visited the year before.

There's a phrase from Zen Buddhism, *sottaku doji*, that describes the point in time when an egg is ready to hatch: the chick pecks at the shell from the inside, while its mother pecks from the outside. In this way, new life arises from both internal and external efforts.

I feel that this book was born in a similar fashion, both from the efforts of those who wished to see the mill's story told, and because the story itself was ready to come out into the world. Both forces coming together at the same time are what finally transformed this story into words. I was present to assist with its delivery, but my role was only that of a guide, taking it from an incorporeal form to words on a page.

And so I found myself in Ishinomaki to do research and reporting.

The people I spoke with seemed to sense my role, and treated me as an archivist there to record and preserve their memories of what had happened. They spoke frankly of their experiences, both the good and the bad. It was as if the time had come for them to tell their tales for the benefit of the next generation.

The story I relate in this chapter is that of the owner of a small pub in the area. To protect his privacy, he asked me to use a pseudonym when relating his tale.

2

Up until the earthquake struck, Mamoru Watanabe owned a pub in the shopping district near Ishinomaki station. A steadfast, charismatic man, Watanabe is well liked by those around him. He is in his mid-forties, but bustling about in his typical uniform of traditional Buddhist work clothes, he seems much younger. His pub was a popular place, thanks to its good atmosphere and delicious food. NPI employees often gathered there.

He never imagined himself to be in danger from a tsunami, yet on the day of the earthquake a black wave ripped through the town, destroying the life he had built up.

Watanabe's first thoughts were of his sons' safety. They were both still in elementary school, and their school was near the ocean.

He set out toward his home, wading through the freezing water. Just in front of a tunnel he had to pass through, however, the water grew much deeper. Peering into the tunnel, he saw only a stretch of black water reflecting light coming in from the other end. The waist-deep water was quickly sapping his body heat. He stepped on something that yielded oddly beneath his boots, and shuddered at the thought of what it might be.

He trudged on, step after step, until the water reached his chest. He stopped, unable to advance further, and silently called out to his family as if that would summon them. Instead, there was only silence and falling snow.

He stood there for a time, overwhelmed with despair and mournful resignation. *If I've lost my children, I don't think I can go on*, he thought. *If they've passed on, I'll have to follow them.*

Normally his home was only a short drive away, but that day a vast distance seemed to separate him from his family. Not being with his children at a time like this was almost too much to bear.

After considering the water for a while, Watanabe gave up on making any more progress. He turned and trudged through the muddy water back toward his pub, pondering what he could possibly do.

His shop was on the second floor of a building and had therefore escaped damage. On the day after the earthquake the city was filled with hungry people, so he gathered ingredients from the kitchen and threw everything into a large pot to make a stew. Keeping busy allowed him to concentrate on what he could do to help rather than obsess about what he couldn't do.

When the gas canisters for his stove were empty he collected bits of wooden debris, dried them as best he could, and used them to build a fire outside. For three long days the waters refused to recede, preventing him from making another attempt to return home.

On the third day another shopkeeper hailed him as he was tending a fire across the street from his pub.

"I saw some guys go into your place," the shopkeeper said. "Friends, maybe?"

"You sure?" Watanabe said. He had just come back from getting some spices inside and hadn't seen anyone. He shrugged. "Guess I should go say hi, then."

He crossed the street and headed up the stairs to his restaurant. It was dark inside, but he could hear people moving around. Something didn't feel right.

He worked up his courage and stepped into the pub. Several men he'd never seen before were inside. Watanabe felt goose bumps break out over his body.

"Who the hell are you?" he said. "What do you think you're doing?"

Surprised by his voice, the men turned his way and froze. One finally spoke. "We've got permission from the fire department," he mumbled.

"You *what*? What are you talking about?"

Watanabe attempted to restrain his anger and keep calm. Looking around, he saw a cut-open bag that had been filled with food. One of the men had his hands on the cash register.

"Get away from that!" Watanabe shouted.

The men turned their eyes from Watanabe, but remained standing where they were for several seconds. Then they meekly filed out of the room, apparently unwilling to escalate the situation any further.

They didn't look like the type to attempt burglary in a normal situation, which only made Watanabe angrier. *What, just because there's no one around to arrest you, you think you have the right to do as you please?* he thought.

Everyone in the city was in the same situation, yet almost all of them were hanging in there, waiting for help. No matter how bad things were, almost no one else had resorted to thievery. Watanabe sneers when remembering them.

For a time, the shopping district became a prime target for burglars. They would wander around with baseball bats and golf clubs, looking for stores to break into. A boutique owner watched as bat-wielding thugs shattered her showcase window. When she screamed at them to stop, one turned and told her to shut up. He and his companions forced their way into the store, gathered up armfuls of clothing, and ran off. Someone broke into a jewelry store and stole several expensive necklaces and watches.

While it had not been damaged as severely as some other parts of town, the area Watanabe was in had become a lawless zone. There was no electricity, no way to make phone calls, and no police to come to anyone's aid. The shopping district had been left to fend for itself.

If men who broke into Watanabe's pub had been neighbors he would have recognized them, so he figured they must be residents of another part of town who had taken refuge on Mt. Hiyori. His neighborhood had been cut off by floodwaters, and they were still waiting for aid to arrive. It was hard to imagine people coming in from far away to steal things, but it was also painful to imagine locals robbing one another. Still, the burglaries continued, shocking and angering the shopkeepers. Watanabe was disgusted, unable to understand how the thieves could live with themselves.

The waters still hadn't fully receded by the fifth day, but Watanabe decided to make another attempt to get to his family across the river. This time, he succeeded. When he finally reached home he found his wife there. She told him their children had taken refuge at school with their grandmother, under the care of their teachers.

Watanabe nearly collapsed with relief. He paused to give a silent prayer of thanks for the teachers who had saved his children, then rushed off to the school. When he arrived, however, his children were nowhere to be seen. A neighbor saw him searching frantically and told him that they had been relocated. Cursing the further delay, he headed off to where they'd been sent.

He finally found them at a shelter with his mother-in-law.

"I don't think I've ever been so happy. I didn't want to ever leave their side again," he says.

When he went back home, his wife delivered some unpleasant news.

"The daughter of a relative was still missing," he told me. "She was just eighteen, and the very day of the earthquake had learned she'd been accepted to college. She'd gone to get her acceptance papers that morning. Later we heard that just when she got home, the tsunami swept her away along with her mother and grandfather. Her life was just starting, and now she was gone."

Watanabe sat down to talk with his wife about what they should do. They felt that the area around their home was becoming unsafe due to crime, so they decided she would join the rest of the family in the evacuation shelter until something more permanent could be found. Watanabe would return to the pub and come back to get them when he found a place for them to stay.

Back in the shopping district, Watanabe helped with cleanup activities. He learned that an acquaintance had lost both his shop and his home. Watanabe offered to let the man and his family stay in an apartment he rented in town. Other people had saved his children; now it was his turn to help someone else. Pulling together in this time of need was the first step toward rebuilding everyone's lives.

He decided to take out a loan and move his pub to a new location closer to his home. Compared to the close brush with death he had just experienced, a little debt seemed like nothing to fear. Besides, the shopping district had been heavily damaged. He and his fellow shopkeepers had been losing patrons since before the earthquake, for reasons including the development of shopping malls on the outskirts of town. The disaster was the final nail in the coffin. Watanabe also wanted to stay closer to his family in the future. He would open a shop near their home and do what he could to help his community.

"I was so disgusted by what I'd seen," he says. "The news was full of all these feel-good stories, but that wasn't everything. I got an eyeful of just how ugly people can be."

He began commuting between his home and Ishinomaki Station every day. He rarely saw anyone on the way, even during the day, but it seemed like those he did see were up to no good. One day he saw several families raiding a convenience store. As he watched, they went in and came back out with armfuls of stolen merchandise, "like they were heading off for a picnic." It would have been one thing if they were simply collecting food to survive, he thought to himself, but they were also carrying cases of beer.

Having a shop destroyed by a natural disaster can be chalked up to fate, but Watanabe felt that having it survive the disaster only to be destroyed by human hands was disgraceful.

On another day he saw a group of men and women gathered around a parked car with a gasoline can, clearly stealing gas.

Later he began hearing ugly rumors. He told me about one of them when we visited a driving range surrounded by a tall net for catching errant balls.

"Rumor was that when the tsunami passed through here lots of corpses got caught up in that net, and that when they were found some were missing fingers. Bodies swell up in the water, right? So looters after jewelry would snip off fingers to get the rings. The rumor was that foreigners were doing it."

After the Great Kanto earthquake in 1923, many ethnic Koreans were killed in attacks inspired by groundless rumors. It was disturbing to see similar stories brewing again, like evil spirits arising from the aftermath of the disaster. It was a sign that people were beginning to distrust those around them. All it took was a loss of electricity and cell phone service to blur the lines between rumor and reality, to make it impossible for some to distinguish between truth and fiction.

Another baseless rumor circulated that NPI was hoarding relief supplies. On occasion, NPI employees who were distributing food were called hypocrites. Someone contacted a city employee to demand that the city confiscate relief goods that "the national government had delivered earmarked for NPI." The employees in the clubhouse were rumored to be holding decadent banquets; in reality, they were living off canned food, like everyone else.

With no electricity, nights were frighteningly dark. Women and children were told not to leave emergency shelters after sundown, and men formed neighborhood patrol groups to keep burglars away from empty homes. They worked on the cleanup during the day and served on patrol duty at night, making for many sleepless nights. Back in the dormitories where the NPI managers were staying, Kurata began sleeping with a baseball bat near his pillow. A very small number of criminals had become an invisible enemy that kept the others afraid of the dark.

As summer came and went, rumors began swirling about those who had received insurance payments. There was talk that the owner of a large chain of local stores who lived in Tokyo had swindled the insurance companies for a huge amount of money. Though the maximum payout was supposed to be 50 million yen (around $500,000) per building, he had finagled things so that he got twice that amount, people said. That was just one of many rumors running rampant.

There was talk of someone using a hose to wet down his home to convince insurance inspectors that the tsunami had hit it, thereby scoring 2 million yen ($20,000). Ruffians were said to be extorting unwarranted insurance payments from civil servants. The general theme of the gossip was that some people had lost everything but were getting nothing, while others more skilled at manipulating the system were making out like bandits.

One day Watanabe received a phone call from the landlord of the apartment he had offered up to an acquaintance as a temporary home.

"We have a problem," she said.

When he rushed to the apartment to meet his landlord, he couldn't believe what he saw. The occupants had created a makeshift bathtub in the middle of the room by piling up concrete blocks and lining the basin with a plastic tarpaulin. They had also nailed up sheets of plywood to create a small room to subdivide the space.

"They'd left things like that and taken off. They even left their own stuff behind. I can't believe that's how they repaid me for letting them stay at my place." Watanabe shakes his head. "Just unbelievable."

Watanabe searched for the family but was unable to find them. Nonetheless, he initiated a lawsuit to recover damages in their absence.

As fall approached, former residential areas began to fill with tall grass and reeds. On most of the lots, barely discernable outlines of foundations were the only reminder of where houses had once stood. Those that remained standing looked almost new from afar, but on approach revealed dark interiors. Storm shutters had been ripped from window frames, and white curtains fluttered in the gaping holes.

Broken bits of crockery and lost toys still littered the ground. Here and there the sky reflected off of puddles that never seemed to dry up. Previously thriving communities were now barren and silent, except for the rustle of wind blowing through weeds.

Given this eerie backdrop, perhaps it is no surprise that strange stories began to circulate.

In one, a volunteer driving over a bridge was said to have stopped for a woman standing by the road. When he asked if she needed help, she said, "Please give me a ride. I'm lost, and I'm not sure where I'm supposed to go." The volunteer felt sorry for the woman and offered her a ride in the back seat. They started off, but when he turned around to check on her, she was gone. According to the story, the Ishinomaki Police Department got so many calls about similar ghost sightings that they shut down that stretch of road.

Another story tells of a facility that was distributing free meals immediately following the earthquake. Those inside refused to evacuate to higher ground, and as they argued the tsunami came and killed them all. When the waters receded they were found tangled together in a narrow stairway. Later, workers tried to clean the building, but reported feeling ghostly hands coming up from beneath the floor and grabbing at their feet. This scared them so badly that they ran from the building and refused to reenter. The city tried to hire companies to do the cleanup on four separate occasions, but each abandoned the job, citing worker injuries. Finally they found the last corpse, caught inside the ceiling.

Watanabe often heard stories like this from his customers. He would smile and nod, knowing that ghost stories were a way of coping with the pain of disaster.

When I met him, Watanabe was managing a fundraiser to collect money to repair local schools.

"Slow and steady wins the race," he said. "Ishinomaki is slowly getting back on its feet, but we're also losing population as folks move on to greener pastures. It's going to be hard for local restaurants. New ones are opening up all the time, but they're mostly the big chains moving in around the station and squeezing us locals out. Still, I was ready to die that day, so I'm prepared to carry on like I've got nothing to lose. I don't care how far I go into debt to do it. If things don't work out, the banks can do with me what they will." Watanabe gives a deep laugh. "Guess we'll see what happens, eh?"

The N6 machine, one of the largest of its kind in the world

CHAPTER 8

Getting the Paper Rolling

1

Some machines at the Ishinomaki mill proved harder than others to bring back online. The digester used to produce chemical pulp was particularly challenging.

The digester is huge, sixty meters tall with a capacity of 920 cubic meters. Wood chips and chemicals are placed inside and brewed at a high temperature and pressure to break down the lignin that holds wood fibers together, leaving only cellulose from which pulp is extracted. Normally the contents of this massive pressure cooker are a liquid, but in the months following the earthquake they had hardened into a concrete-like substance.

This wasn't the first time a digester had been out of service for a long period. The digester at a plant in Indonesia once broke down for several days, but when staff opened the manhole-sized port on the side of the tank they discovered that the contents hadn't yet hardened—a jet of the stuff spewed out in a thirty-meter stream, coating a nearby building.

In Ishinomaki, however, the pulp slurry had hardened and nobody knew how to get it out. As far as anyone knew, the situation was unprecedented worldwide. With water mains to the factory still unrepaired, employees tried wetting the slurry down with water from a fire hydrant, but it was like spraying a stone—the water bounced right off.

The team tasked with fixing the digester began to panic. At the request of team leader Yukio Suda, technical division director Akira Kanamori asked Kurata for permission to try something unusual.

"We might be able to excavate it from within. Would it be okay if we tried to get somebody in there?"

Kurata shook his head. "No way."

Given the no-holds-barred approach Kurata had taken when the electrical team was trying to procure wiring, Kanamori knew he was willing to approve extreme measures. He also suspected that getting workers into the tank would make the task much easier. But worker safety had to take priority over expediency.

When pulp rots it can create hydrogen sulfide, a heavier-than-air gas that smells like rotten eggs. Breathing it interferes with respiration and can cause fainting or even death. The slurry in the digester appeared to have hardened completely, but that wasn't certain; a thick top crust could be concealing a pool of liquid, and if it collapsed under the weight of workers they would fall through and almost certainly die. Even if no one died, a serious accident would put a stop to all operations, throwing everyone off schedule.

"Kurata chastised me for even considering the idea," Kanamori says. "He told me that safety always comes first, that we couldn't let anyone get hurt, no matter what."

For their next attempt at resolving the situation, the team brought in two vacuum trucks. One blew high-pressure air onto the hardened pulp to try to loosen it, while the other sucked out anything it could from the porthole on the side. Progress was excruciatingly slow: after a full day, only a few centimeters of pulp had been removed.

Twice Suda went directly to Kurata asking for permission to let someone try climbing in, but Kurata was adamant. Instead, he created a graph, charting the team's daily progress.

"See? It's taking time, but you're getting there. There's still time before we need to have the digester up and running, so you'll make it. Just keep doing what you're doing."

Years ago Kurata had promised himself that if a fatal accident ever occurred under his watch, he would take responsibility and resign. No scenario justified putting expediency before human life. The staff had just survived one of the worst natural disasters in recent history; allowing anyone to die in an industrial accident now would be a tragedy too weighty to bear.

Suda and the others on the digester team continued clearing out mud and debris during the interminable wait for the vacuum cars to do their job. Mud was everywhere, from floors to drainage systems, and much of it had to be removed by hand. Clouds of flies rose up from disturbed piles of debris. The team made flytraps by putting honey in plastic bottles, but in just two days the traps became so clogged with flies that they were rendered ineffective.

2

The Machine 8 building had been inundated with two meters of water, and that water had brought with it an unbelievable amount of debris. To meet the tight recovery deadlines, cleanup and equipment recovery efforts had to be performed side-by-side.

The first floor housed most of the electrical equipment and motors, and dedicated cleaning crews were working feverishly to make their deadline of getting everything spic and span by September. Engineers needed to work in the same space at the same time and had their own tight deadlines. Inevitably, clashes arose regarding who would get to work in an area at a given time. The teams held careful negotiations to work out schedules that would allow them to attain their shared goal of getting everything running again.

On many days Ikeda from the electrical department worked until dawn. Shimura from the procurement division worked alongside him, repairing pumps and other mechanical devices. Over one hundred pumps needed to be fixed and tested before they could be used again.

"The ones on the first floor were bad enough," Shimura says, "but there were also pumps down in the pit below the first floor. As you'd expect, the pit was full of water and so dark and muddy we couldn't see into it. We had to scoop all that mess up, and the whole time I dreaded finding a body. I freaked out one day when it looked like a hand had floated up to the surface, but it turned out to only be a glove.

"There were pipes full of rotting pulp, which produced hydrogen sulfide. Somebody got hold of detectors, and we had to clip those onto our clothing. When they detected hydrogen sulfide they'd sound an alarm and we'd clear out so nobody would get poisoned."

Shimura's pregnant wife had temporarily relocated to Yamaguchi prefecture, at the extreme western tip of the main island of Japan.

"She was staying with relatives. When they mentioned her situation to somebody at city hall, the local government there gave her a cash gift to help us out. That was such a kind gesture."

Shimura was working a schedule unimaginable under normal circumstances, but he has no complaints.

"There were plenty of folks who couldn't get to work every day, either because they'd lost family or for some other reason. We had to cover for them if we were going to get the machines running again, but that's okay—my family and my home were safe, and I was receiving relief supplies, so it didn't seem right to complain or slack off. It was a hard time, but I just slugged through it, letting inertia carry me forward instead of dragging me down."

3

Nearly half a year after the earthquake, Machine 8 manager Noriaki Sato was still unable to sleep well. Getting Machine 8 running again would be the mill's first step toward recovery, and the pressure weighed heavily on him.

Sato's bosses knew how finicky their "spoiled princess" could be, and asked him not to go on any long business trips. Members of his team joked that Machine 8 would throw a tantrum and break down when he left, only to start working smoothly again as soon as he entered the room. "If we're going to get this thing working, you'll have to be standing next to it," one said. Sato was willing to do whatever it took.

The team decorated Machine 8 with the paper cranes that the Machine 7 team had folded for them. Soon, bundles of paper cranes began arriving from other factories, too. Each crane represented a prayer that echoed Sato's: *Please, come back to life.* Sato half believed Machine 8 had a soul; if it did, then surely these prayers would reach it.

Kurata was on tenterhooks. Above all else he wanted to achieve his goal of restarting production in six months, showing both the company and the world that the Ishinomaki mill was on its way to recovery. Getting Machine 8 running again would be a huge morale booster, proving to his employees that all their hard work was paying off. It would also show people outside the company the amazing work they were doing.

On September 14, 2011, Machine 8's operators were ready to try starting up the device for the first time since the tsunami. The digester still hadn't been fully cleaned out, but workers were able to start up the main machine all the same.

Around one hundred factory employees, representatives from headquarters, and visitors from NPI-affiliated companies crowded into the building that housed Machines 7 and 8. Sato was determined to make the day into a grand celebration that witnesses would remember.

"I wanted it to be like a festival," he says. "I wanted everyone to walk away knowing that the factory was making a comeback and that Ishinomaki was still strong. We cleaned everything as best we could and decorated the room with all the paper cranes we'd received. We did everything we could to put people in a celebratory mood. We didn't feel like we were only doing it for the company. This was going to be a shot in the arm for the entire region."

Even under normal circumstances, getting a 111-meter-long sheet of in-production paper running through a paper machine is no small task. Threading a sheet from where it is first formed at the initial wire mesh through to the spool at the end takes at least one hour, and often longer. The smallest irregularity can cause the paper to tear, requiring the whole process to be started again.

Sato recalls a similar day before the disaster, on the first run after some upgrades. "We just couldn't get a full sheet threaded, try as we might. We started out with a roomful of people, intending to cheer with a big *banzai* when everything started running, but we started losing spectators in dribs and drabs. By the time we were good to go, all that was left was a thin crowd of people whose jobs were directly connected with the machine. I really didn't want to see something like that happen again."

Everyone on the team was nervous. The machine hadn't run for half a year now, so who knew what problems might arise? Kurata and a few other executives scattered some ceremonial purifying salt and offered up a cup of sake to the feeder machine that supplied the paper machine with raw materials.

Japanese papermakers treat their machines not as physical objects, but as living entities with souls. They never walk in shoes on the paper their machines produce, even discards that will be thrown away. Doing so would be a betrayal of the deep love and respect they have for their machines.

The employee acting as master of ceremonies picked up a megaphone and addressed the crowd: "And now, Mr. Kurata will press the button to start the feed pump!"

If all went well, the NPI Ishinomaki mill would, with that action, once again begin producing its "Highland" brand, a staple product it had been making for many years.

Kurata went to the control panel, festooned in red ribbons, and pressed a button. The huge, old machine released a deep groan and slowly rose from its slumber. The sounds it emitted were so loud that conversation became difficult. Yet they were music to the ears of those who knew them well.

Nozzles began spraying a white cloud of pulp onto a wire mesh, which moved slowly to create a sheet.

At several "goosenecks" along the paper's windy route, human operators had to manually feed the paper to its next destination. At each of these points a long, thin tube appeared and blew air against the paper to press it against the reel around which it would be wound. An operator directed the tube's long nozzle at the delicate sheet of paper to help guide it into position. The task required timing, experience, and no small amount of skill. Threading the paper through the entire machine to the final reel is a difficult task that even experienced operators don't always get right on the first attempt. They pulled it off that day, however, and paper began flowing smoothly through Machine 8 with impressive ease.

The spectators, who had come prepared to wait for hours, began buzzing with surprised excitement. An employee from the public relations department at Tokyo headquarters scurried about with a camera, taking photos of the paper as it made its 111-meter journey through the machine. The rest of the crowd followed him as he made his way to the end of the production line.

The area in front of the drying reels was filled with the roar of hot blown air and the metallic clanking of countless spinning rollers. The air was hot and moist, causing the operators and spectators to break out in a sweat. The paper passed into a size press, which applies a starch coating, and then into another dryer. It then disappeared into the calender section, where it would be pressed to give it sheen.

The crowd gathered around the final reel grew larger, and Sato felt himself quiver with excitement.

"We'd lost family in the earthquake and tsunami. A big part of the community we lived in too," he told me. "I hope we never have to live through times like that again. But there's one thing I'm thankful for—that this horrible experience showed me just how wonderful something as commonplace as making paper can be."

Sato gave a signal, and Fukushima pressed the button to begin winding the paper onto its massive exit reel. With another whoosh an air cutter sliced away the paper, which wound around the reel with a noisy rustling.

"The paper is threaded!" Sato shouted.

The crowd responded with applause and cheers. No one had ever heard of a threading being completed in less than an hour, but today they had set a new record: just 28 minutes.

Sato, overcome with emotion, made his way to the edge of the crowd. He gave Machine 8 a silent thanks: *You pulled through for us. Thank you. You're amazing.*

A coworker found him and dragged him back in front of everyone, demanding he address the crowd. The MC shoved the megaphone into his hands.

"Can we have a word from you, Mr. Sato?"

The machine operators nodded and looked at Sato. He scanned their faces. They were haggard after the long, hard months of work, yet they retained a look of determination.

Sato wiped his eyes on the sleeve of his work coveralls. He raised his arms and shouted the only word he could think of, with all his might:

"*Banzai!*"

The others joined him.

"*Banzai! Banzai!*"

Kurata, Fukushima, and the machine operators all had red eyes. No doubt the emotions they felt—some combination of regret, sadness, joy, stubbornness, and pride—can be fully understood only by those who took an active part in the recovery. But whatever they were, their shared feelings made words unnecessary. The men celebrated the machine's recovery with firm handshakes and slaps on the back.

The Machine 8 operators gathered around Sato, lifted him up, and threw him high up in the air over and over again as they cheered.

It was quiet outside the Machine 8 building, where Ikeuchi from the electrical department and Shimura from procurement had paused to look up at the steam rising from a chimney. There weren't many people out, but an employee from headquarters who happened to be passing by stopped to talk to them.

"You aren't joining the celebration?" he asked.

"No time," Ikeuchi said. "Too much backstage stuff to take care of."

The man nodded silently and gave Ikeuchi a friendly slap on the shoulder.

"Thanks for what you've done," he said. "It's guys like you that have made this possible."

Shimura smiled at the unexpected compliment. *Good to know somebody's paying attention to everything we're accomplishing here*, he thought.

Shimura's son had been born earlier that month. Being raised in Ishinomaki would mean growing up along with the city's recovery. He would be a beacon of hope for all those around him.

4

As soon as the book publishers heard news of Machine 8's recovery, the orders started rolling in.

Shueisha came first with an order for the paper used to print their bestselling comic titles *One Piece* and *Naruto*. Employees at the mill recalled the copies of these comics that Shueisha had donated to children in the region and the handwritten notes of encouragement that they had contained. *It's good to be able to do business with them again,*

Sato thought.

Machine 8 purred along, seemingly happy to be making paper again.

Nobutoshi Yabuno from Tokyo headquarters contacted Machine 7 team leader Noriaki Sato with an interesting proposal: perhaps they could create a new product to produce on Machine 8? They co-developed a paper and named it "b7 Bulky." When they showed it to Yabuno's boss, Shinichi Sato, the response was immediate:

"This is amazing. This will absolutely sell."

NPI staff had been working for many years on the problem of how to produce paper with more bulk. The easiest way to create cushiony, high-bulk paper is by mechanically grinding the wood chips. However mechanical pulp still contains lignin, which causes paper to discolor easily. That doesn't happen with chemical pulp manufactured in a digester, but the tradeoff is a paper with lower bulk. Bulk can be increased simply by using more pulp, but that makes the paper too heavy to appeal to readers.

Working with the chemical manufacturer Kao Corporation, NPI found a way to use surfactants such as detergents to loosen the bonds between wood fibers. Mixing the surfactants with pulp produced the light, fluffy effect they were after.

A second problem remained, however. The surface of high-bulk paper tends to be rough, preventing it from taking ink well. This renders it unsuitable for printing photographs and diagrams because they cannot be reproduced in detail. One solution is to apply thick coatings that smooth out the roughness. Softness is sacrificed, however; the paper becomes overly stiff, like a shirt with too much starch.

Shinichi Sato recalls the day NPI hit on a solution to this problem. Publishing sales manager Tomoh Kaneko was hunched over his desk, staring intently at something.

"What are you up to?" Sato asked.

"Check it out," Kaneko replied, holding up a vial of liquid.

In the vial was kaolin, also called China clay, dissolved in water. Kaolin is used in various products, including porcelain and cosmetics. Kaneko poured a little onto a sheet of paper and used a ruler to smooth it out. As the liquid dried, a residue of powder adhered to the paper in a thin layer, giving it a natural finish.

"Look how thin this stuff goes on," Kaneko said.

That was the birth of "b7 Cream," a high-bulk coated paper for book publishing. (The "b7" refers to the guitar chord; Kaneko was an avid guitar player and included the term as an allusion to harmony.)

Holding the samples Yabuno had brought, Sato felt the same excitement he had felt the first time he saw b7 Cream. Yabuno's b7 Bulky was similar, but thicker and lighter. It still had b7 Cream's excellent photograph reproduction qualities—photos almost seemed to leap off the page—and as an added bonus it had a non-glossy finish. The paper was also a true white, with no hint of yellow, blue, or red tinting.

"This is going to be a hit, no question," Shinichi Sato said.

He was right. Six months later, NPI was selling over 1,000 tons of b7 Bulky per month. To put this in perspective, the paperback edition of the bestselling Japanese novel *Forever Zero* sold around four million copies, requiring approximately 1,300 tons of paper.

At first b7 Bulky didn't have many buyers, but before long publishing executives and designers caught on to its virtues. The product soon became a popular selection for accent paper in magazines and for books that contained photographs. Today it is Machine 8's most popular paper.

Fukushima from the Ishinomaki mill laughs and says, "We had our problems with the sales department, but they promised to work as hard at selling our paper as we did to get the plant running again. I guess I'll have to forgive them."

5

Removing the hardened pulp from the digester took 106 days, and was finally completed on October 26. The task had required an enormous amount of time and money, but worker safety was not compromised.

However, Suda's work wasn't finished. The 1KP (for "kraft process") digester that he manages produces the pulp used by the massive N6 Machine, so Suda would have to restart that digester before N6 could start up again. The goal was to restart the N6 machine by March 11, exactly one year after the earthquake. The pressure was difficult for Suda to bear.

In January his team tried running water through the 1KP digester. Unfortunately that winter was a particularly cold one, and the water froze. Work ground to a halt as Suda and his team researched ways to thaw the ice.

Finally, in February of 2012, Suda's team managed to get the digester working again. The one-year anniversary of the disaster was just a month away.

6

Haruo Noguchi, manager of the N6 Machine, was born and raised in Ishinomaki. His parents had lived in a section of town that was completely destroyed by the tsunami, and the first floor of his own home had been washed out, making it unlivable. Ever since the earthquake he had been moving from place to place—shelters, friends' homes, company dorms. Nevertheless, he maintained his lighthearted air, and speaks with a tinge of humor.

"To be honest, the delayed schedule for N6 helped out a lot," he says. "I had no idea when I'd be able to get my house fixed, and I was renting a dorm room. It was all I could do to get my life in order. The N6 Machine is on a completely different scale from the others. When I heard they wanted to get a machine running in six months I thought, no way, not the N6. Things looked okay up on the second floor, but all the electrical stuff downstairs… The N6 pretty much runs itself, but that means it's a really complex system. You can't go halfway in repairing a machine like that. Fixing all that in six months? I don't think so."

Noguchi had wanted to find a job at the Ishinomaki mill right out of high school, but the company wasn't hiring at the time. Instead, he took a job at a local car dealer. He finally got a job at the plant when he was 23 years old. Later he completed both a mid-level management course and a college degree by attending night school while employed full-time. Perhaps it is no surprise that he also pulled through the year-long grind of getting such an enormous piece of machinery running again after the tsunami.

He almost didn't succeed. Tests performed on the N6 Machine on March 6 didn't go well, and Noguchi and his team ended up spending three straight days and nights trying to fix the problem.

"We were using shower sprayers to clean all those rollers, but the water was so dirty the nozzles would clog. Funny thing was that Machine 8 and the N4 were guzzling down water with no problems, so we figured the issue must be within the factory, not with the municipal supply. On the 6th we installed equipment to filter the water, but on the 7th something was still causing the paper to split in the machine. That was kind of a rough day. We'd already announced that we'd display the machine running on the 9th and had printed up advertisements and all. It would have been so embarrassing if we didn't make it."

Indeed, a demonstration of the machine in action was supposed to be part of citywide ceremonies to mark the one-year anniversary of the disaster. The mayor of Ishinomaki was scheduled to attend, along with CEO Haga and many reporters.

"I could see the head of the factory, Mr. Kurata, watching us from the control booth. His expression was growing darker and darker as time went on. It was a little scary, to tell the truth."

Noguchi says that Kurata can be a tough boss to work for, but that "he understood what we were asking of these machines. I knew he was on our side."

The problems continued. They were getting a ribbon of paper, but it was full of holes.

The N6 machine produces the thin, soft paper used in catalogs and advertisements at twice the speed of Machine 8. Even when functioning properly its paper rips easily. Now, vertical holes were developing in the middle of the paper and immediately widening until the sheet tore completely.

The N6 machine has a high-performance suite of diagnostics equipment. According to that system, the rips were developing in the dryer unit and widening when the paper came into contact with the long blade that spread the coating agents. The machine operators weren't sure why that was happening, but they decided to start by addressing the symptoms. Since the initial hole was appearing in the dryer unit, they tried gradually adjusting its settings. Paper that is too dry rips more easily, so they increased the amount of moisture retained.

Noguchi crossed his arms and stared at the machine as yet another test run began. The paper passed the coater without ripping and continued through to the end.

Later Noguchi and his team crawled under the dryer with flashlights and peered into the machine's guts to find what was causing the rips. They discovered a tiny screw wedged into a groove on the cylinder face, extending just a few millimeters above the surface. Apparently it had fallen from the ceiling on the day of the earthquake. That tiny protrusion had been enough to weaken the paper it came into contact with.

"Well, I guess we found it," Noguchi said, rolling the silver screw on his palm. He picked it up between two fingers and dropped it into a pocket. This was his third day spent without leaving the N6 building.

Noguchi paused to watch the N6 Machine, which had been turned back on and was now humming along making paper. He recalled the long hard days since the earthquake—the cold and the heat, the stench of decay and clouds of flies, the weight of the mud he'd helped haul out of the building, trudging up and down the hill day after day in work gear... All of these experiences were indelibly etched onto his body and soul.

Now the recovery that for so long had seemed like a dream was materializing before him.

The goal was in sight, but he wasn't there yet. Busy days still lay ahead. *Better get to it*, he thought.

On March 26, 2012, CEO Haga pressed a switch on the N6 machine, and NPI's "monster" groaned into motion. The enormous machine is capable of producing 350 thousand tons of paper per year. As a sheet began streaming from its end and began tightly spooling onto the receiving reel, a cheer arose from the crowd of onlookers.

Thanks to the timing of the event, the story was picked up by newspapers and television programs throughout Japan. NPI had incurred around one hundred billion yen (US$1 billion) in damages, mostly related to the Ishinomaki mill. The only private company with higher recovery costs was the Tokyo Electric Power Company, owner of the disabled Fukushima Daiichi Nuclear Power Plant.

In commemoration of the first year of recovery efforts, author Seiichi Morimura penned the following haiku:

We remember this
earthquake so that our wounds will
not fester, but heal.

NPI's Ishinomaki paper mill announced its
full recovery on August 30, 2012

CHAPTER 9
The Finals

1

After coming so close to qualifying for the Intercity tournament in 2011 and 2012, the NPI Ishinomaki baseball team had high hopes for the 2013 season. Unfortunately, things got off to a bad start.

Even before the Intercity tournament preliminary matches began, the team suffered an embarrassing three straight losses in the Tohoku regional tournament. Their second loss to 2012 Intercity champions JX Eneos was particularly painful—JX beat Ishinomaki by scoring a grand slam home run.

"Nothing like that to take the wind out of your sails," says Coach Kimura with a wry smile.

The team finally broke its losing streak in the first round of the Intercity preliminary games, playing against the JR East Tohoku Company. That game was saved by Takuya Koike, who came in as a pinch hitter in the eighth inning.

Koike had been on the Ishinomaki team since before Kimura became coach. Although not as flamboyant a player as many of those scouted by Kimura, he was a familiar face for many employees at the Ishinomaki mill. Every morning he could be seen swinging a bat or jogging near the company dorms.

With the crack of his bat during that game, the Ishinomaki fans in the bleachers jumped up and began cheering his name. His hit not only brought home a tying run, it also jumpstarted the rest of the Ishinomaki batting lineup, which went on to score four more runs for a 5–1 comeback victory.

Ishinomaki wasn't the only team that had come to the Intercity tournament with an appetite for victory, however. After a series of one-point-margin wins and losses, Ishinomaki was barely hanging onto a spot in the series. That's when they lost in extra innings to Kirayaka Bank from Yamagata prefecture, an up-and-coming team that had garnered a number of good players in recent years.

Normally that would have spelled the end of their shot at the Intercity title, but they were given a second chance through a unique feature of the Tohoku preliminaries—the wild card. Under this rule, the second-place finisher among the three tournament blocks with the best win–loss record is promoted to compete in the final tournament.

This peculiar rule saved the Ishinomaki team.

Their first game was once again against Kirayaka Bank. Losing to them for a second time was not an option. Although Ishinomaki trailed Kirayaka through the fifth inning, star hitter Ryota Ito finally found his groove and kick-started the batting lineup into action. A fierce series of hits followed, as if the Ishinomaki team was venting its frustration at not being able to play to its potential over the previous few years.

The Ishinomaki fans went wild. Back in the dugout Coach Kimura smiled with satisfaction. *Looks like the baseball gods are finally smiling on us*, he thought. As the game progressed his players rounded the bases as if a weight had been lifted from their shoulders.

Ishinomaki went on to defeat Kirayaka Bank 6–4. They also won their next game against the TDK Corporation, putting them in the Intercity tournament finals for the second time in the team's history.

The 2013 Intercity tournament finals were held in Tokyo Dome on July 17. Ishinomaki faced the Shinetsu Baseball Club, from the city of Nagano. The Ishinomaki team drew over ten thousand fans, so many that they overflowed their designated area adjacent to third base and spilled into the stands behind left field. Everyone waved light blue balloons—the team's color—and an enormous fisherman's flag decorated the infield stands.

One section of the stands was occupied by megaphone-wielding cheering teams from two NPI-affiliated sales agencies, Shinsei Pulp & Paper and NP Trading Company. Both had been sending cheering squads to tournaments that Ishinomaki played in for decades. Also in the stands was a young NPI employee relaying play-by-play reports via his computer to those in the company who couldn't make the game. The game was also being broadcast by a Tokyo television station, which was using the Ishinomaki team's success to symbolize the recovery of the Tohoku region.

Back in Ishinomaki, the local FM radio station was covering the game live, allowing residents to hear for themselves the excitement in Tokyo Dome. The mill's raw materials division manager Urushibata, a former team member, was providing commentary for the broadcast.

In the bottom of the first inning Ishinomaki gave up one run but recovered it in the top of the second. The tie was short-lived, however— Shinetsu scored twice when they came back up to bat. The game was not off to a good start.

But this was not the same team that had failed to qualify for the Intercity tournament the year before. At the top of the third inning Ryota Ito came to bat with one out and runners on first and third. His home run put Ishinomaki in the lead, and the team went on to make an amazing seven base hits for a total of six runs batted in in that inning alone. With each hit the Ishinomaki fans cheered with such fervor that the stands shook, and the cheering squad's rendition of the team song echoed off the dome's high ceiling.

Oh! Oh, Ishinomaki! Your time has come!
Oh! Oh, Ishinomaki! Now is your chance!
This is the day we've been waiting for!
Go forth and fight for Ishinomaki!
Our victory cheers will ring
in the blue skies over the Kitakami River!
Oh! Oh, our Ishinomaki!

One of the fans in the bleachers that day was Masahiko Kondo, the salesman from the Kansai office who had delivered the first reports of Ishinomaki's fate to NPI headquarters on March 11. Since then he had been transferred to Ishinomaki and had taken the day off to attend the game. Between cheers for each hit and swallows of beer, he would shake his head in amazement. *I can't believe this day has come.*

Noriaki Sato, leader of the Machine 8 team, was also in the stands. To his surprise, he ran into a familiar face from the days immediately following the tsunami.

"You're the bicycle guy!" a man said to him.

"You're the spinach guy!" he replied.

"Of all the people… What a coincidence."

"Thank you for your help that day. That coffee probably kept me from freezing."

Back at the factory, excited employees gathered around radios tuned into FM Ishinomaki, celebrating each run with cheers and applause. They listened in as Aihara relieved Aizawa as pitcher and proceeded to shut down the Shinetsu Baseball Team for Ishinomaki's first-ever win in an Intercity Baseball Tournament finals match.

The second game in the series was held on July 19. Ishinomaki faced off against JFE Steel, from western Japan. Aizawa stayed on as starting pitcher. In the bottom of the second inning, Yoshitaka Goto hit a double, bringing one runner home for an early lead. He advanced to third, then on to home in a squeeze play by Kegoya for another run. A timely hit by Ito brought in two runners, raising Ishinomaki's lead to four points. The stands shook with cheers and waves of balloons in a sea of blue.

Kimura laughs when recalling the game. "Ito had actually been in a slump all season. I guess he was saving himself for that day."

In the seventh inning Takashi Goto, the Waseda University graduate who had so thrilled Japan in the 2006 Japanese High School Baseball Championships, was finally pulled off the bench he'd been warming. "Get out there," Coach Kimura said.

Finally, my time has come, Goto thought as he trotted onto the field. His heart danced as he heard co-workers shouting his name in encouragement. Playing baseball—especially playing baseball for others' enjoyment—was the best feeling in the world. Things hadn't been easy since he joined the team in 2011, but now here he was in Tokyo Dome, its bright lights casting his shadow onto the vivid green artificial turf. NPI's cheering squads were up in the stands, cheering for *him*.

In the top of the eighth JFE Steel managed to narrow Ishinomaki's lead by one point, but it wasn't enough. Ishinomaki fended off further gains, and took the win.

The team went wild. The tournament ended there for them, but for the first time in the club's history, they had finished the season as a Top 8 team.

Coach Kimura had done amazing work with the team in just five years, but at the end of that season he hung up his jersey and retired. He was joined, without fanfare, by Waseda graduate Takashi Goto.

2

Six months later, Goto reappeared in the sales division of NPI's Tokyo headquarters as a newsprint salesman. He had traded in his baseball uniform for suits and striped business shirts, and instead of rounding bases he was learning how to make the rounds of important NPI customers.

"I'd been mostly just playing baseball for twenty-some years, so at first it felt like a part of me had been ripped out," he says. "But I'd always known that I couldn't keep playing ball forever, so I was mentally prepared for the change. Now I'm focusing on work. The market for newsprint is shrinking every year, so it's kind of a tough business to be in. But I figure that if we made it through the earthquake and tsunami, we'll find a way to pull through this slump too."

Hiromi Kurata retired from his position as head of the Ishinomaki mill in September 2012 and now works as a consultant from his new home in Chitose, Hokkaido. He says he's enjoying the more laid-back lifestyle there, which allowed him the time to pen *538 Days of Triumph and Despair*, an account of his experiences during the disaster.

"At first I thought about visiting schools and places like that to talk about what happened, but it's too painful to relive over and over through the telling. Writing it out once was all I could manage. Should I ever find myself in the same situation again, I don't think I could pull through," he says.

Like a veteran of war uncomfortable on his return to peaceful lands, Kurata says he sometimes feels uneasy in cities untouched by the disaster. So far, time has not dimmed his memories or softened the pain of his experiences as he hoped it would. Once when speaking with an employee who had been transferred from Ishinomaki to Asahikawa, he said, "It's almost like we were somehow sick back then, isn't it? And that sickness still hasn't quite left our hearts."

Kurata says his emotions are difficult to put into words, especially when speaking to people who did not live through the disaster. Not that he blames them for not understanding; he remembers the Great Hanshin Earthquake of 1995 and how distant that disaster felt to him at the time.

When Kurata heard that the Ishinomaki baseball team would be playing in nearby Aomori, he got on his motorcycle and rode down to watch. The team won the game, putting them into the 2013 Intercity tournament. When the game was over, he went to pay his respects to coach Kimura.

"Thanks for all you've done for us," Kurata said.

"I'm the one who should be thanking you," Kimura said, wiping away a tear. "If I didn't have baseball to pull me through, I don't know what I would have done."

When I ask Kurata what he thinks about the future of the paper business, he says, "Well, it isn't a rosy picture. The market is shrinking along with the population, and people are reading fewer books these days. It's hard to be optimistic."

Kurata believes NPI will be forced to scale down as Japan's population and economy as a whole shrink in coming decades. Paper companies in other Asian countries are becoming formidable competitors as they acquire machines on the scale of the N6. Plus the trend toward the digitalization of books can only accelerate, he believes.

NPI pulled through the Great East Japan Earthquake, but the paper industry is still on shaky ground. As Kurata says, it's hard to be optimistic about the future. The future of Japanese paper companies will be determined largely by the fate of the nation's industrial sector, the fate of the Tohoku region, and the fate of Japan itself.

I ask Kurata what he thinks the secret to survival will be.

"Well, that's up to the newspaper and publishing industries," he replies. "When they sell their products, we sell ours. Publish good books that will sell. It's all up to you guys."

And so the baton has been passed.

The task is not an easy one. According to the 2014 Annual Report of Publishing Indices, approximately 4.18 billion books and magazines were printed in Japan in 2000. By 2013, that number had fallen to 2.44 billion. Sales of printed material aren't so much descending a slope as falling off a cliff.

To hold a book in your hands is to hold the end product of a long series of events that started in the forests of Australia or South America or Japan's Tohoku region. Skilled craftsmen and women transformed those raw materials into paper, editors did the same to polish the text printed on them, and bookbinders and printers used their knowledge of paper to produce the finest finished product possible. Only after all of these steps are completed does a book appear on the shelves in bookstores. The book you hold is a manifestation of the skill and dedication of many people whose names you will never know and whose faces you will never see.

Each book has a unique design and binding. Open the cover of this book, for instance, and turn its pages. You'll find that the paper has a certain tautness, but not so much that it loses its softness. The paper is bulky, yet light. It has an off-white tint that was carefully determined by the book's creators. Pages showing photographs retain their softness yet reproduce the photos in vivid color.

Today, Machine 8 is still producing paper, and Noriaki Sato is still at its helm. I asked Sato and his daughter Ayana what was so compelling about producing paper at the Ishinomaki mill to warrant the extraordinary efforts poured into its recovery.

"There's something I often tell the people who work for me: Imagine a kid in a bookstore, clutching his allowance in his fist. He's come because he's going to spend that money on a comic book. *That's* who we're making paper for," Sato says.

"Did you ever notice how kids never get paper cuts when they read comic books? All those soft little hands turning all those pages, and it never happens, thanks to what we do. When you make paper thicker it gets stiffer and more likely to give you a paper cut. So we've found ways to loosen the bonds between pulp fibers in a way that thickens the paper while retaining its softness.

"They say the paper industry is in decline, but there will always be a need for paper," Sato continues. "As long as I'm around, I won't let it die out. When I give my kids the last book I ever do in this life, I want it to be printed on paper, not on some damn memory stick. I used to take Ayana to the bookstore and proudly show her all the books I'd helped make. 'Pretty cool, huh?' I'd say. Then she'd say—"

Ayana smiles wide and finishes her father's line.

"I'd say, 'Yeah, Dad. Books are wonderful.'"

Epilogue

Finishing up work on my final day in Ishinomaki, I put on my coat and left the office I'd been using. When I stepped outside, the cold seemed to penetrate to my core. I looked up and saw a brilliant column of steam against a deep blue evening sky.

A white van was waiting for me outside the office. A driver in work overalls stepped out and opened the door for me. I took one last look around, trying to fix the image of the factory in my mind. The huge digester loomed behind me. I recalled Noriaki Sato referring to Machine 8 as a spoiled princess, and I realized that after having spent so much time talking to the workers here the entire plant now felt like some enormous living thing.

I bid Ishinomaki a silent farewell and climbed into the van.

The driver slid the door shut with a rattle and a bang, and for a moment I was ensconced in silence. When the driver rejoined me he offered to take me to the Sendai train station, and I thanked him. From the back seat I heard the ticking of the turn signal, and we left the factory grounds. The hum of the engine and gentle shaking soon made me sleepy.

The driver spoke: "So where are you from?"

"Yokohama," I said. "Are you from around here?"

He nodded. "We used to have a house near the sea, but…you know."

"I see." I looked at his hands on the steering wheel. "Where were you when it happened?"

"I was waiting in a car near the Ishinomaki City Hall while Mr. Murakami was in a meeting."

"Wait, so you're Mr. Sugawara? The driver who brought Mr. Murakami back to the mill after the earthquake?"

"I am. I was sitting in the car when the quake hit. I've never felt shaking like that. I couldn't hear any sirens or anything, just all this loud banging. Turns out part of a wall had collapsed and hit the car. I was afraid I'd be crushed, so I pulled into the city hall parking lot. Mr. Murakami was coming out just as I arrived. He told me to take him to the plant, so I turned right around and came back. Nobody was on the road, so we got back in no time."

I recalled what Murakami had told me of the events of that day. It was fascinating to hear Sugawara's side of the story, fitting in like a puzzle piece. After Murakami got out at the factory gates, he'd told Sugawara to take the car, get his family, and meet up with everyone on Mt. Hiyori.

"Was your family okay?" I asked.

"They were, thanks. I got my mother and wife into the car, along with two neighbors. We made it up the mountain just in time. They wouldn't have made it otherwise. Mr. Murakami saved their lives."

"I'm so glad to hear that."

We fell silent for a time. I watched the scenery passing by outside my window. Wide lots remained empty where houses had once stood, and there were no lights in the area.

"We hurried up the hill, but we never thought a tsunami big enough to destroy our house would hit," Sugawara said. "We left everything there, didn't bother to take any valuables. One of our neighbors did turn back partway, saying she'd forgotten something important. We never saw her again. I think she must have been washed away with her house."

"I'm so sorry."

"My son's wife made it up the hill too. She drove to the kindergarten that's up there. That car was the only possession they were left with. I remember another woman we knew who went back to get things just before the water came. She ran upstairs, but the water made it that high. She was only saved because she got sandwiched between her house and a neighbor's. A helicopter picked her up, she said. There are so many stories like that. Of course, we only hear about what happened to those who survived."

We turned onto the two-lane road that led to Sendai station. It was backed up with cars heading the same way. The rice paddies and mountains surrounding me were growing darker. Looking out the front window, I saw a long line of taillights snaking off into the distance—a traffic jam caused by construction to widen the road.

Sugawara continued his tale.

"The refuge site was a mess at first. No power, no water, no gas… When we finally got our first ration it was one-third of a banana. I guess it was about a week before the first relief supplies started showing up—rice balls and the like. The elementary school had power by then, so even people whose houses weren't damaged would come by to use the electricity. They'd bring electric pots to boil water to make instant ramen in one of the classrooms. The smell of that ramen, I tell you… Never before have I wanted something so bad. Luckily, food started trickling in soon after. After a while we got so much that families of five were getting rations for eight—somebody had to eat it, after all.

"Even after the food was worked out, living arrangements were rough. After a few days I was able to rent a place from NPI, but it was me, my wife, my mother, and four people each from our son's family and our daughter's, all living there together. Everybody was in a similar situation, but still—having that many people under one roof isn't easy. Take the baths, for example. Imagine what a tub of water looks like after eleven people have been in it. As soon as the Self-Defense Forces set up communal baths, we started using them.

"I remember one night it was raining and so, so cold. My mother is pretty old, and at the time she was already blind in one eye. We were afraid she'd slip and fall or catch pneumonia or something, so we told her to stay home while we all went out for a bath. So of course she decides to try to bathe herself, in this unfamiliar place, and somehow ends up falling and landing face-first on the faucet. Now she's blind in both eyes.

"I wanted to get into one of the prefabs they were setting up as soon as possible, but they were allocated by a lottery system and my number wasn't coming up. I heard they were trying to prioritize families with elderly people in them, but we were still one of the last to get a place. We were in the NPI rental for five months. It was October before we finally got public housing.

"Not long after moving, my wife started feeling sick. We took her to a small clinic around November, and they told us that she needed some tests. We didn't get the results back until December—that's when we found out she had pancreatic cancer. She was going to have to undergo chemo for a while, leaving no one to watch after my mother, so we started looking for a home for Mom to move into. The poor woman was 85 years old, and she'd been moved from the house she'd lived in most of her life to a shelter at a school, then to company housing, then to prefab housing for evacuees… If she'd been able to stay at home she might have been able to cope with her vision problems just by groping her way around, but even in the tiny place we wound up at she didn't know where anything was.

"We finally found a home for Mom at the end of December, and my wife started chemo just after New Year's. She started losing weight right away, and in less than a month she was skin and bones. I figured what we needed was our own house to live in—big, small, I didn't care, just some place that was our own. We started building a small, single-story house that my wife could get around in, but… Well, it was too late.

"Every day since the tsunami had been a battle, and now this. I was sixty years old and I'd never fixed a meal for myself. When I was younger I was a truck driver, and after that I drove tour buses. I'd be away for days, sleeping at hotels, and when I finally got home she'd be there, waiting for me with a hot dinner ready. She was my anchor.

She took care of all our finances too, so I didn't even know how much money we had, or where it was.

"Right through until the end, she never complained about the pain. She'd just talk about how worried she was about other people. She'd come home from treatments and I'd tell her to take it easy and get some rest, that I'd get dinner somewhere before I came home. She'd just say, 'Oh, don't you worry about me. They gave me a shot that fixed me right up. Get home when you can—I'll have dinner waiting.' Not once did she complain about side effects of all those drugs."

"She was a good wife," I said.

"She was indeed. Better than I deserved," Sugawara said. His smile showed even more than his words the depth of his feelings for her.

"Right until the end she kept insisting that she could look after my mother. She was adamant that the new house would have a room for Mom, so it does. Of course now she's living alone, and I'm alone too. It's not a very comfortable place. It's never really felt like home to me, more like I'm staying at a hotel. I guess now I'm paying the price for not learning how to be more self-reliant when I was younger. It almost makes me feel bad about what Mr. Murakami did for me—he saved my life, but now I'm not sure I have a life worth saving."

I thought about what Sugawara's life would have been like now had the tsunami never come—his and the lives of all the other survivors whose fates were shuffled around by that wall of water.

"My wife was only in the hospital for about ten days," Sugawara continued. "I visited her every day after work, and our daughter would take over after I'd gone home. One night she called me and said my wife was having trouble breathing. I told her it was late, that she should get home, just to tell the nurse before she left. The hospital called me around ten that night to tell me that my wife had passed away. She was gone when they went to check on her. I can't believe I let that happen, let her die all alone like that. Thankfully they say she must have passed quietly—there was no sign that she'd thrashed about or was in distress."

We entered Sendai with its tall buildings and beautiful bright lights, twinkling as if the earthquake had never been.

"That last day, when I was getting ready to leave her, my wife smiled at me and said, 'You take care of yourself, now. Don't catch cold.' Those were her last words to me."

I reflected on the weight of that which the dying leave behind for those who will remain.

"You never know what life will bring you, I suppose," Sugawara said.

"You never do," I agreed.

I looked out the window, watching the buildings pass by as I searched for the right thing to say. I ended up remaining silent for the rest of the trip.

We arrived at the Sendai train station. Coming from the dark place I'd been in, the bright lights made it feel like midday despite the late hour. As I was getting out of the car Sugawara came around to help me with my bags. I bowed and thanked him, then turned to head for my train. As I walked away, Sugawara called to me.

"Ms. Sasa!" When I turned around, he was smiling. He said, "I hope you can come again! Next time I hope we can talk about more pleasant things. I'm sure there will be more enjoyable conversations next time you're here."

I waved to him as I searched again for the right words. There was plenty I should have said, but the best I could come up with was, "I will! Thank you, and best of luck."

I headed for the escalator that led to the train platforms, turning back to bow and wave as I did. He remained where he was, to see me off. As I moved away he grew smaller, fading into the crowd until I could no longer see him.

References and works cited

Books:

Kurata, Hiromi. *Zetsubo To Kando No 538 Nichi: Higashi-nihon Daishinsai Nipponseishi Ishinomaki-kojo Fukko no Kiroku* (538 Days of Triumph and Despair: A Record of the Great East Japan Earthquake and the Rebuilding of the NPI Ishinomaki Paper Mill).

Nippon Paper Industries, Ishinomaki Mill. *Shinsai No Kiroku* (Records of the Earthquake).

Nippon Paper Industries, Ishinomaki Mill. *Shinsai No Kiroku, Shiryohen* (Records of the Earthquake, Archival Edition).

Nippon Paper Industries, Ishinomaki Mill. *Fukko No Kiroku* (Records of the Reconstruction).

All Japan Magazine and Book Publisher's and Editor's Association Research Institute for Publications. *2014 Nenban, Shuppan Shihyo Nenpo* (2014 Annual Report of Publishing Indices).

Websites:

Tohoku Regional Bureau Ministry of Land, Infrastructure, and Transport. Ishinomaki Minamihama District Memorial Park Basic Proposal Reference Materials. http://www.thr.mlit.go.jp/bumon/b06111/kenseibup/memorial_park/miyagi/common/file/miyagi_sankoushiryou_01.pdf.

Gendai Business. *"Follow-up on the stars of the Waseda and Komazawa Tomakomai teams, seven years after the Japanese High School Baseball Championship Rematch."* http://gendai.ismedia.jp/articles/-/36535.

Diamond Online. *The heartbreaking story of the tragedy at the Okawa Elementary School.* http://diamond.jp/category/s-okawasyo.

Article:

Sakai, Kuniyoshi. "No O Tsukuru 'Shoten' ("Book stores" build brains)." *Kotoba Magazine,* issue 11, April 2013. Shueisha.

About the Author

After graduating from Waseda University's School of Law, Ryoko Sasa became a Japanese teacher, and then a nonfiction writer. She is noted for her research of the Kabukicho area of Shinjuku, Tokyo. Based on that experience she wrote *Kakekomidera no Gen-san* (Gen-san, a Man Who Devoted Himself to an Urban Shelter) in 2011. In 2012 she was awarded Shueisha's Takeshi Kaiko Award for Nonfiction for her book *Enjeru Furaito* (Angel Flight), about international funereal repatriation teams.

（英文版）紙つなげ！彼らが本の紙を造っている―
再生・日本製紙石巻工場

Saving the Mill: The amazing recovery of one of Japan's largest paper mills
following the 2011 earthquake and tsunami

2015年3月27日　第1刷発行

著者: 佐々 涼子
訳者: トニー・ゴンザレス
発行所: 一般財団法人 出版文化産業振興財団
〒101-0051 東京都千代田区神田神保町3-12-3
電話: 03-5211-7282（代）
ホームページ: http://www.jpic.or.jp/

印刷・製本所: 大日本印刷株式会社

*The full square kilometer of the NPI Ishinomaki
Paper Mill grounds*

A shot taken by cameraman Taiji Takashi as he ran from the tsunami. The photo shows the mill's front gates at 3:48 PM, just after the tsunami swept in.

Scenes of the recovery

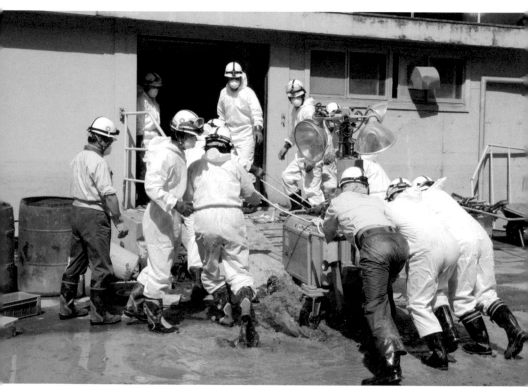

Staff from the procurement division moving portable spotlights into the Machine 8

Motives division staff removing debris

Workers inspecting the coating and cutting room

Debris and spools of paper in the No. 2 Coater building

A street in Ishinomaki the day after the tsunami

After the disaster

The coating inspection room

After debris removal

The mill's front gate

A road on the plant grounds, covered with pallets, wood chips, and logs

The Number 8 Paper Machine, which produces paper for hardcover and paperback books, comics, and other kinds of paper for the publishing industry

The N6 machine is one of the largest paper machines in the world and can produce 1000 tons of paper per day.